# Plays By
# Jeffrey M Jones

**Broadway Play Publishing Inc**
New York
BroadwayPlayPub.com

Plays By Jeffrey M Jones
© Copyright 2000 Jeffrey M Jones

All rights reserved. This work is fully protected under the copyright laws of the United States of America. No part of this publication may be photocopied, reproduced, stored in a retrieval system, or transmitted, in any form or by any means, electronic, mechanical, recording, or otherwise, without the prior permission of the publisher. Additional copies of this play are available from the publisher.

Written permission is required for live performance of any sort. This includes readings, cuttings, scenes, and excerpts. For amateur and stock performances, please contact Broadway Play Publishing Inc. For all other rights please contact the author c/o B P P I.

Cover photo: Peter Cunningham

First printing: December 2000
I S B N: 978-0-88145-183-2

Book design: Marie Donovan
Copy editing: Sue Gilad
Typeface: Palatino

## CONTENTS

*Dedication* .................................................. *iv*
*About the Author* ............................................. *v*
*What the Hell Was I Thinking?* ............................... *vi*
*Acknowledgments* .............................................. *x*
TOMORROWLAND ................................................... 1
THE CRAZY PLAYS .............................................. 77
THE ENDLESS ADVENTURES OF M C KAT ........................... 167

# DEDICATION

These plays are for Page, and eventually Camila and Mason, because I love you all so much.

## ABOUT THE AUTHOR

Jeffrey M Jones' other plays include A MAN'S BEST FRIEND, DIRTY LITTLE SECRETS; PUSS-IN-BOOTS; J P MORGAN SAVES THE NATION (score by Jonathan Larson); LOVE TROUBLE; WRITE IF YOU GET WORK (score by Dan Moses Schreier); CRAZY PLAYS QUE FUMAR; ANNUNCIATION WITH WRANGLERS; OFFICEWORK; WIPEOUT; DER INKA VON PERU; 70 SCENES OF HALLOWEEN; NIGHTCOIL; and THE FORTRESS OF SOLITUDE. He is currently an instructor at the Yale School of Drama.

# WHAT THE HELL WAS I THINKING?

Once upon a time, when I was young, I decided I would make a name for myself by blowing up the play form. It never occurred to me to ask whether anyone wanted the play form blown up and this, in hindsight, may have been a mistake—but that's another story. I wanted to make Weird Theatre, clearly the most interesting kind of theatre one could make, and being of an academic bent, decided the most rigorous way to make Weird Theatre was to see how much of the play form could be blown up.

Then around 1983, as I recall, I got stuck. I'd somehow lost the ability to make up dialog for my characters, and this was not a happy moment. In desperation, I started plagiarizing words for my dialog from *other* writers, and of course never intended to show the results of my plagiarization—at first. I even tried to make up for the fact I was plagiarizing by using only writers who were very bad, or at least whose words were never intended for the stage. But as time went on, you know, I got more and more interested in cutting and pasting and plagiarization, and finally made a collage play called DER INKA VON PERU which I liked very much and which you may still be able to find in a book called *Seven Different Plays* (Mac Wellman, ed.; and put out, once again, by Broadway Play Publishing Inc).

Collage exists in the space between coherence and nonsense. It relies upon our instinctive propensity toward making sense of things if at all possible as a way of engaging the spectator to infer meanings which are relatively free of the author's control. Through collage, I stumbled upon two insights I might otherwise have never had: That because stories have parts, it is possible to substitute equivalent parts of quite different stories and still make a kind of sense; and that when an actor says something which doesn't quite follow from the last thing, our tendency is to infer some private thought as the cause, thus replicating our real-world experience of other people with their hidden thoughts, and thereby making the stage character that much more interesting.

DER INKA was supposed to be about a lot of things, but to me it was ultimately about a kind of history—specifically, about ideas of history and historicity (this because so many of the texts had an overt historical context—which is to say, they were about a time or embodied a sensibility—over and above their actual context within the history of English literature). Unfortunately, I also knew this brilliant thesis was apparent to me alone. In fact, I had to admit that audiences had been a little *put off* by what they saw as an implicit challenge to identify the sources of my texts (which, since so many of the sources were junky, was bound to be a fruitless effort, but of course, *they didn't know that since I hadn't told them*). So in setting out to write what I was already calling my second Historical-Quotation play, I decided first to concentrate on an historical period which would be immediately recognizable (the 1950's) and second, to use only texts which wouldn't call attention to the question of their sources. This second play turned out to be TOMORROWLAND, and it contained only material from the films, magazines, newspapers and advertisements of year 1950.

1950 was a regular Jubilee Year of paranoia (the Russians not only having exploded the H-Bomb but Klaus Fuchs having revealed the espionage that gave them those secrets, to say nothing of the start of the Korean War) *but also of the Good Life*—side by side: T V *and* Polio. Frozen Food *and* all kinds of creeping menace in godforsaken Asian hellholes. Body Odor *and* the Friendly Atom. To read a popular magazine like the *Saturday Evening Post* was to ride through a bizarre funhouse, where one page screamed of impending catastrophes (even your innards might betray you *unawares!*) while the next held out promises of endless bounty on easy terms. Perhaps the most interesting and surprising discovery was a recurrent figure in the Westerns of that year: a Southerner in Western Territory (where, significantly, American law didn't really apply), either during or shortly after the Civil War, living outside the established community patrolled by the Union Army, and thus a man whose allegiances were immediately suspect. This character appeared in different guises in movie after movie—sometimes in league with the Indian, sometimes merely hated and feared by the Army command; sometimes betraying the established order (though usually with cause), sometimes merely sacrificing himself to preserve that order. And it was through this motif that I discovered, for the first time, the American cowboy.

For the record, I'd had no interest in the cowboy as a kid except as a pretext for the gunfighter game. The point of this interesting game was to die as slowly and splendidly as possible, and while the basic game was highly codified (you had to say "awwwww" and sometimes "Ya got me!" when you were hit, and clutch your side; nobody ever got shot in the eye or the kneecap or squeezed off a fatal round as they were going down or blasted the enemy away with a shotgun or turned out to be merely wounded) it was nonetheless a point of pride to have introduced some novelty—some new stagger, spin, flip, flop or crawl which might have come from last night's GUNSMOKE or WANTED DEAD OR ALIVE or HAVE GUN WILL TRAVEL or THE RIFLEMAN or whatever your parents let you watch, and could be executed even better off a *diving board*... TOMORROWLAND turned out to be the start of my ten-year romance with these murderous cowboys. They just kept getting dumber and dumber and faster and faster (or slower, as you will see), and I always found a way to tuck them into some spare corner of the landscape—until at last I wrote a play about Mr J P Morgan, where there was no room for them any more. Which is called the Closing of the American Frontier, and is another story, too.

Cowboys are hard for actors, by the way. They don't know much about 'em nowadays, and their first tendency is do character cowboys with funny voices, like Festus or Gabby Hayes—perhaps half remembering John Wayne, who also talked funny (thought not like that). In fact, cowboy heroes almost *never* talked funny, unless you count Jimmy Stewart's stammer or Coop's halting croak or even, god help us, the mannered flutings of an Errol Flynn as "funny." For a lot of us back then, the *ur*-Cowboy was still the voice of Matt Dillon on the *radio* GUNSMOKE— who turned out, much later, to be the fat detective Cannon on T V, played by William Conrad. But that's really another story. Thinking about it now, I believe the real problem of getting the cowboy voice right has to do with amplification. You need to be able to speak in little more than a mutter and still fill up a vast landscape—which, if you're not in a movie, can probably only be done on mike. Try it and let me know, I'm curious.

There was another play after TOMORROWLAND named WIPEOUT, also cut up, this time from Plato and Homer and the American Independent Beach Movies, but it's not in this book so we don't need to talk about it. Then came THE CRAZY PLAYS, which have their own Afterward, so we don't need to talk about them either. But I was pretty darned proud of THE CRAZY PLAYS, because I figured I'd blown up the play form just about as good as anybody could and still have something to show for it. Unfortunately, I also had to admit that audiences hadn't had a ton of fun at the CRAZY PLAYS. In fact, I realized it had been years since I could recall an audience having fun at Weird Theatre. From this I sadly concluded that Weird Theatre was a Back Number and Extinct, and thenceforth resolved to write only silly plays.

Now when my wife, Page Burkholder, graduated from medical school her supervisor gave her a little stuffed figure of a meerkat (she did this for everybody, by the way—all her charges got their own little animals, what can I say?). So we're having a celebratory dinner that night in a restaurant, with my ninety-year-old godmother and Jim Clayburgh and his wife Sylvie and this *meerkat*, and I made some kind of crack about the meerkat, whereupon Sylvie fixed me with her sky-blue eyes and said, with the aplomb God grants glamorous Frenchwomen, "Oh, Jeff, you are so silly—don't you have a stuffed animal?"

Friend, if you did not know it, there turns out to be an entire substratum of society which has its stuffed animals, and these animals lead pretty darned interesting lives, too. In time our little friend, now M C Kat, had his own share of adventures (admittedly with some assistance from Page and me), including getting lost in a Tuscan landscape, and it occurred to me to wonder if an animated creature who got along so well(?) in the world couldn't find his way on stage. Which he did, of course, first in THE ENDLESS ADVENTURES, and subsequently in a musical entitled WRITE IF YOU GET WORK, which isn't in this book either.

Here is all you need to know about working with the Kat. First and foremost, the Kat is not a puppet. The Kat is a stuffed animal—and a commercially manufactured stuffed animal at that. (Unfortunately, the Smithsonian Institution—source of the original—no longer sells the little guys. This play was also written before Timon gave performing meerkats a bad name and spawned a new line of merchandise. Just do your best. Something will turn up.) Puppets are illusionistic and require skill. A stuffed animal, on the other hand, is a *plaything*. Any kid would know how to work M C. That kid would just hold him out in front of herself and start talking—to the Kat, with the Kat, as the Kat—it's all the same.

You can improve on this if you like—you'll find that cocking his little head, for example, makes him appear to be "interested"—but there are really only two basic schools of meerkat performance: The Paleface sees herself as a mere operator, and insists that the creature always have a surface to stand on. Make sure there are plenty of waist-high counters and table tops and fences on the set, and explain—when she wonders who she is when she's speaking—that she's his Guardian Angel, or something. The Redskin, on the other hand, will do just about anything she damn well pleases with the creature, and then ask you to explain M C Kat's motivation. Either way, they'll both want the prop at the end of the run, so buy extras.

The only point of THE ENDLESS ADVENURES OF MC KAT is to make your audience feel sadness at the death of a stuffed animal. Such is the weirdness of theater that this is possible.

Finally, the dull stuff: There are some typographic conventions in the text which may warrant explanation: Line breaks indicate whole thoughts which generally correspond to single phrases; line wraps (indents) indicate the continuation of the same line. Ellipses (...) indicate thoughts and phrases left trailing; parentheses indicate spoken comments which are intentionally *not* directed at another onstage character, including conventional asides as well as private phone conversations, overheard whispers and so forth. I have included ground plans and stage directions to let you see how *I* did these plays, which is not to say that *you* should do them this way. A continuous musical underscore, however, is an extremely economical and powerful way to make collage text more "meaningful;" and the firecrackers used in TOMORROWLAND, while totally illegal, leave a really neat smell of gunpowder in the air.

## ACKNOWLEDGMENTS

I am profoundly indebted to the actors who gave these words life—especially those who came back to do so time and again: Karla Barker, Zach Grenier, Gary McCleery, Hugh Palmer, Mary Shultz, Liz Schofield, Barbara Somerville, Victor Talmadge, Damian Young, and of course Zivia Flomenhaft, who really was in everything. I am forever grateful to the artistic directors who gave my work a home: Liz LeCompte, Greta Gunderson and Richard Caliban. Special thanks to Dan Moses Schreier, from whom I learned so much, and to the creative teams who let these plays live on: Patty Lynch and Bruce Charlesworth; Tim Farrell and John Wellman; Dennis Zacek; Jean Randich; Melanie Dreyer. And finally, love to you, Dad.

# TOMORROWLAND

*A History of Western Philosophy
by W T Jones, Vol. II*

TOMORROWLAND was originally produced by Creation Production Company, opening on 6 September 1985 at the Performing Garage in New York. The cast and creative contributors were:

TELEVISION STAR SHANNON MALLESON (*also* HUDRAY) ......... Karla Barker
DIVINA WILFRED (*also* MISS PEGGY) ................... Barbara Somerville
JASON WILFRED (*also* JIMMY RINGO) ........................ Zach Grenier
SELDEN CLARK (*also* FRANK JAMES) ....................... Gary McCleery
CAROL WILFRED (*also* MRS KENNISTON) ................. Zivia Flomenhaft
DR CLIFF SINCLAIR (*also* LIBDER *and* DOC) ................. Victor Talmadge

*Direction & set design* ....................................... Jeffrey M Jones
*Sound* ................................................. Daniel Moses Schreier
*Costumes* .................................................. Catherine Zuber
*Lights* ..................................................... Jeffrey McRoberts
*Assistant direction* ............................................... Jon Larson
*Stage management* ........................................... Brad Phillips
*Assistant stage manager* ....................................... Mary Bolton

## NOTE

Virtually all dialog in this play has been constructed out of source material dating from the year 1950. Interested producers are hereby advised that certain texts used in this play may be protected by copyright law.

Permission for use of the sound score in this text must be obtained by writing Daniel M Schreier, 34 N Moore Street, #4E, NY NY 10013. All music indicated in the score is also obtainable from the same address.

DELRAY BEACH...just a typical Florida town,

...until the sun goes down....

...then it's NEIGHBOR AGAINST NEIGHBOR,
with BLAZING TORCH and LASH and HANGMAN'S ROPE!!!

Men and women
dedicated
to what was to become a Lost Cause:

JASON WILFRED (A K A JIMMY RINGO)—a head for figures...
...and a SUSPICIOUS MIND...
CAROL WILFRED (A K A MRS KENNISTON)—just an ordinary housewife...
...OR IS SHE?
DIVINA WILFRED (A K A MISS PEGGY)—she's behind the eightball...
...AND SHE DOESN'T EVEN KNOW IT!
SELDEN CLARK (A K A FRANK JAMES)—Varsity quarterback, dream date...
...AND TROUBLE!
DR CLIFF SINCLAIR (A K A LIBDER and DOC)—he thinks the Health Dept
needs to know a lot more...*ABOUT EVERYONE!*
TELEVISION STAR SHANNON MALLESON (A K A HUDRAY)—she's out of this
world...*IN MORE WAYS THAN ONE!*

...so won't you join us as we visit:

the OFFICE of Dr Cliff Sinclair...
the SUNPORCH of the Wilfred's magnificent, new 1950 home...
and through the sunporch window, *the MOON, with the Earth rising!*

*(Sound: "Tomorrow Tone")*

*(The performance space is separated from the house by a pipe railing four feet high running the full width of the seating risers at the foot of the first row. White wall units twelve feet high divide the performance space into three areas.)*

*(The DOCTOR's office is defined by a six foot wall, set nine feet upstage parallel to the pipe rail, stopping three feet from the extreme stage left edge of the performance space to create an entrance. A small wood desk is placed in the center of the office; the doctor's chair faces the audience upstage of the desk, the patient's chair is downstage left of the desk, facing onstage. There is a microphone stand on the doctor's desk.)*

*(The sunporch of the WILFRED's beautiful, new, modern home is the main acting area. Stage left, it is defined by a six foot wall running upstage from, and perpendicular to, the onstage edge of the doctor's office. Four feet further upstage, a twenty-four foot wall runs parallel to the pipe rail, nineteen feet upstage of it, stopping five and a half feet from the extreme stage left edge of the performing space. A third wall extends six feet downstage perpendicular to the stage right edge of the second wall; a fourth wall extends four feet off stage right from the downstage edge of the third wall, running parallel to the pipe rail, stopping three feet from the extreme stage right edge of the performance space to create an entrance. The room is furnished with a table and four chairs center, fifteen feet upstage; and an easy chair eight feet upstage of the pipe rail, centered on the stage right wall. There are three place-settings at the table, S L, S R, and up center. A second microphone feeds from S R entrance.)*

*(The window is an aperture in the upstage right corner of the room, running from two feet to seven and a half feet high, extending eight feet towards center in the upstage wall, and two feet downstage of the corner in the stage right wall. Six feet upstage of the window are two masking units set at right angles, parallel to the corner of the room. The onstage unit, parallel to the pipe rail, is covered with a photomural showing earthrise from the surface of the moon. The other unit is covered with mylar and runs downstage from the stage right edge of the photomural, creating a mirror image.)*

*(Sound: a few minutes before curtain, as the audience is seated, SHANNON speaks over S R mike.)*

SHANNON: Gyro control and compass O K...batteries all off...autopilot O K...everything's in order...pilot's ready...straight ascent from starting point...starting thrust using all tail assembly engines, 2300 tons...fuel mixture: hydrogen and oxygen plus A12, after 120 seconds hydrogen and oxygen plus A14, after 340 seconds hydrogen plus A16, after 560 seconds A16...

Radio and gyro compass in order...automatic pilot ok...fuel consumption normal...air pressure 15 pounds...

Stand by to turn...

Stand by...

4, 3, 2, turn...90 degree turn completed...ship on level flight...speed 3400 miles an hour...altitude 360 miles...three tenths of five left in tail section...

R X M calling Corplum...

R X M calling Corplum...

Hudray speaking...

We have leveled off at 360 miles altitude and are circling the globe at 3400 miles per hour. We will increase speed gradually until we reach escape velocity at 25,000 miles per hour. Everyone aboard ship well. Over to you...

5500 miles...continue acceleration...6,200 miles per hour...altitude 1600 miles...speed 21,000 miles per hour, constantly increasing...check pressurizing system and oxygen...

Boy, this kind of weather makes me feel right at home....

24,000...stand by...25,000...prepare to jettison tail system...start the front assembly motors...forty second supply of fuel left...hold on tight, everybody...

R X M calling Corplum over to you...

We're on our way....

We have jettisoned tail section and are now reducing power and speed according to plan until we come within the attraction of the planet. This is probably the last radio contact before return flight, everybody aboard well....

R X M calling Corplum...R X M calling Corplum...over and out...

*(Sound: crossfade to "Tomorrow Tone Long" and swell lights: fade to black)*

# PROLOG

SHANNON: *(On mike)* And now—
Let us turn the clock forward to the Robot Era of 2150....

With peace and reason ruling,
With vast numbers of highly developed robot machines
And with plenty of atomic and solar energy available,
What would life be like then?

*(Lights up in window. Window: flying saucer descends from S L to S R.)*

SHANNON: The Sahara and other great deserts of today would be fruitful farmlands,
Irrigated by atomic energy and robot water services.
Humans would be happier, healthier, more energetic,
Living an abundant and secure life, with their wants satisfied cheaply by robot factories.
With a turn of the dial, the airwaves will become their servants,
Carrying entertainment from all corners of the world into their homes.
And almost every morning, winter or summer,
Jason and Carol Wilfred will waken to sunlight streaming through the pale-gray and aqua bedroom
Of their Delray Beach, Florida, home....

*(Room: lights reveal* JASON *in easy chair, reading the* Saturday Evening Post; DIVINA *is beside him on the floor, her head on the chair's arm. Sound: crossfade to "Lullabye")*

## Scene One

DIVINA: Daddy?

JASON: Yes, angel?

DIVINA: What is a Cold War?

*(Room:* JASON *looks up from his reading, at audience.)*

JASON: *(Out)* Well, dear,
This odious phrase is used to describe a condition of enmity in which opponents are struggling with each other by every means except armed struggle;

Each, meanwhile, arming with ever more powerful weapons in anticipation of attack from the other,
And in the hope of deterring through fear such an attack.

DIVINA: But how does such a condition arise, Daddy?

JASON: It arises, dear,
When each believes—correctly or incorrectly—
That the other has ambitions incompatible with its own security and way of life.

DIVINA: Oh...

(*Sound: swell "Lullabye," then fade back. Room:* DIVINA *crosses to floor center, studying; then turns back to* JASON.)

DIVINA: Daddy?

JASON: Yes, angel?

DIVINA: Is that belief under present circumstances justifiable?

JASON: Apparently so, angel.
Soviet Communists have always maintained,
And apparently sincerely,
That there will be no security for the Soviet Union so long as any—

(*Sound: crossfade to "Gunfight"*)

JASON: —powerful part of the world remains capitalist—which,
In modern Soviet terms,
Means non-Stalinist.
The Soviet Union is therefore compelled by its basic theory to indulge in perpetual struggle with the non-Communist world....

(*Room: fade lights. Window:* SELDEN *as* FRANK *enters S R crossing center, followed by* CAROL *as* MRS KENNISTON. *Sound: "Gunfight" swell, then fade.*)

## Scene Two

SELDEN: We lost em!

CAROL: Yeah, but you can't stay here, Frank—they'll be flushing these woods!
Can you ride?

SELDEN: Yeah, sure...

CAROL: Ah, no you can't!
You're hurt, Frank—you're hurt real bad.

(*Window:* SELDEN *turns to* CAROL.)

SELDEN: I'll be all right, Mrs Kenniston.
I think we better scatter anyway—
Best thing is every man for himself.
Best thing you can do is draw them away from here.

(*Window: he crosses S R away from* CAROL.)

CAROL: We're in this together, Frank—we stay together.
Must be a thousand posse men swarming this country!
You've got to hide out until things clear up a bit.
You're going to need a lot of care, and you can get it here.

(*Window:* CAROL *crosses to* SELDEN. *Sound: fade out "Gunfight"*)

SELDEN: Maybe you're right.
But how about the people here in this place?

CAROL: They think I went in to town shopping for the day.

SELDEN: That was smart....

CAROL: Be dark in a couple of hours...

(*Window:* CAROL *supports* SELDEN; *they exit S L. Sound: fade in "Mood 2"*)

CAROL: Come on, Frank—take it easy...

(*Room: lights reveal* JASON *&* DIVINA *as before.*)

## Scene Three

DIVINA: Daddy?

JASON: Yes, angel?

DIVINA: Does scientific evidence make it appear likely that the hydrogen bomb can be made?

JASON: Well, dear,
The hydrogen bomb is theoretically possible.
The principles underlying it have been known to scientists here and abroad
For a number of years.

DIVINA: Do we know whether the Russians are working on the hydrogen bomb?

JASON: We have no reason to doubt they're working on all types of atomic weapons, angel.

DIVINA: Do we know if the Russians have produced the hydrogen bomb, Daddy?

JASON: I'm sorry, angel—
To answer that question would not be compatible with national security.

DIVINA: Well,
Do we know how advanced the Russians are in the development of the hydrogen bomb, Daddy?

JASON: Same answer, dear...

*(Sound: swell "Mood 2", then fade)*

DIVINA: Daddy?

JASON: Yes, angel?

DIVINA: Is there a danger that the hydrogen bomb could pollute the earth's atmosphere?

JASON: No...

*(Sound: "The saint" button covers cut from "Mood 2" to "Slow Remorse." Room: fade lights. Window: SHANNON as HUDRAY enters S R, crossing S L while observing a hand-held "instrument." Presently, CLIFF as LIBDER enters S R.)*

## Scene Four

CLIFF: How are the others?

SHANNON: I think everybody's going to be all right.
Fortunately, the engines were turned off before we crashed.
I must have turned the levers off when I blacked out.

CLIFF: But at what speed?
You know the consequences of a body moving with unchecked velocity in free space!

SHANNON: So...?
We made a little detour.

CLIFF: How long has it been since—

SHANNON: I'm afraid we'll never know, Libder; but I've located them.

CLIFF: What?

*(Window: SHANNON crosses to CLIFF.)*

SHANNON: Corplum and the moon.

CLIFF: Well—where are they?

*(Window: SHANNON hands CLIFF "instrument.")*

SHANNON: Take a look.

CLIFF: But, Hudray, it can't be!
The instruments must have gone crazy!

SHANNON: No, Libder...I don't quite know how to tell you, but...

CLIFF: Yes? Yes?

SHANNON: Libder, if I could even have dreamed
That an incredible set of circumstances,
Each precisely and exactly timed,
Would carry us unerringly through space to our most congenial planetary neighbor,
Poskon—

CLIFF: Poskon?!

SHANNON: No doubt whatsoever...

*(Window: CLIFF crosses down S L.)*

CLIFF: But, Hudray...what does it mean?

SHANNON: It means, Libder, that there are times when a mere scientist has gone as far as she can.
*(Window: she crosses down center.)*
We must pause and observe respectfully while something infinitely greater than ourselves assumes control.
I believe this is one of those times.

CLIFF: We shall go on, of course?

SHANNON: Certainly, we shall go on!
We should be betraying an unprecedented opportunity to do otherwise.
*(Window: she crosses S L upstage of CLIFF.)*
A day here is more valuable than years of research on Corplum.

CLIFF: Yes—of course, you're right....

*(Window: as SHANNON exits S L, CLIFF turns to follow. Offstage, CAROL screams. CLIFF exits S L. Sound: CAROL's scream, miked, covers cut from "Slow Remorse" to "Tomorrow Tone." Room: lights reveal JASON and DIVINA as before.)*

## Scene Five

DIVINA: Daddy?

JASON: Yes, angel?

DIVINA: Did you ever kill anybody?

JASON: Nope.

DIVINA: Not even in the war, Daddy?

JASON: Just snakes...

*(Room: CAROL enters in bathrobe and curlers. Sound: CLIFF over S L mike)*

CLIFF: "Disturbed Building..."

CAROL: Jason?

JASON: Yes, Carol?

CLIFF: *(On mike)* "Patients cared for in this building will be chronically disturbed,
Periodically uncooperative,
And assaultive on occasion...."

*(Room:* CAROL *points out window.)*

CAROL: There are creatures out there....

CLIFF: "Suicidal tendencies will be common,
And exceptionally close supervision will be necessary...."

*(Room:* JASON *rises, starts toward* CAROL.*)*

JASON: Are you sure you want Divina to hear this, Carol?

DIVINA: That's all right, Dad—I was just leaving.
*(Room: she exits quickly S R.)*

CAROL: Look...I'm not making this up—
I tell you, I saw them!
Right out there!
And when I yelled, they disappeared....

JASON: All right, Carol
*(Room: he exits S L.)*
Let's go see, shall we?

*(Room:* CAROL *crosses upstage to window; lights fade.)*

CAROL: ...And last night,
Things were answering me...

*(Sound: swell "Tomorrow Tone" Room:* CAROL *steps back from window as, Window:* JASON *crosses S L to S R with flashlight. Sound: "Thomas" button covers cut from "Tomorrow Tone" to "Jazz Offbeats." Office: lights up as* CLIFF *enters, with mike, to rail.)*

## Scene Six

CLIFF: Hello, everybody!
My name is *(Your name here).*
In the story you are about to see,
I play the part of Doctor Cliff Sinclair,
Of the Delray Beach, Florida, Health Department.
*(Room: he sits on edge of desk.)*

The French *voyageur*, Jean Nicolette, was the first white man to come to
   Delray Beach—
That was in 1634.
Today, it is a flourishing business community in the heart of Florida's
   vacationland,
Noted for its paper manufacturing and cheese,
And famous to millions of Americans as the home of the Green Bay Packers.
Of course, our story is completely fictional,
And did not actually happen in Delray Beach,
Or anywhere else, for that matter.
Yet we came to Delray Beach in search of authenticity....

*(Room: follow-spot picks up SHANNON as she enters S R, with mike, crossing behind chair down center to rail.)*

SHANNON: That's right, Cliff—
And during our stay, we fell in love with the small-town atmosphere,
The wonderful year-round warmth and sunshine,
The informal friendliness of the people.
Hello, I'm Television Star Shannon Malleson—

*(Sound: "Applause" button. Room: SHANNON, at rail, crosses S R.)*

SHANNON: And on behalf of the entire company,
We salute the little community of Delray Beach,
And its citizens, who became our family....

*(Room: CLIFF and SHANNON point upstage to CAROL, who turns down from window in darkness.)*

CAROL: Family was large dark animal come roaring down the middle of...
My friends love books passionately...
Every kiss is fine....
*(Room: she exits S L.)*

CLIFF: A big family, Shannon,
That believes in the American way of life.
Folks that have never pulled down an 'Iron Curtain'
Between their hearts
And the Christian ideal called 'Brotherhood of Man'....

*(Sound: "Applause" button. Office: CLIFF sits behind desk, mike in stand.)*

CLIFF: So now, let's set the stage for our first Close-Up:
A Close-Up on Mr and Mrs Jason Wilfred
In their Delray Beach, Florida, home.
Shannon—Mrs Wilfred's your assignment.

*(Sound: crossfade from "Jazz Offbeats" to "Mood 2")*

SHANNON: All right, Cliff—fine.

*(Room: lights up as she crosses up to corner of window and sits on the sill, speaking into mike.)*

## Scene Seven

SHANNON: Yes, almost every morning, winter or summer,
Jason and Carol Wilfred waken to sunlight streaming through the pale-gray and aqua bedroom
Of their Delray Beach, Florida, home.

*(Room: CAROL, in housedress, enters S L and places salad bowl on table.)*

CAROL: It's the magnificent new 1950 home,
Beautifully decorated by Macy's,
The World's Largest Department Store.

*(Room: SHANNON rises as CAROL crosses to easy chair and sits.)*

SHANNON: From the hibiscus hedge comes the song of the mockingbird,
And the scent of gardenia drifts headily in the window.

CAROL: Because today,
The enjoyment of beauty is everyone's privilege.

*(Room: SHANNON crosses center, upstage of table. Office: lights fade.)*

SHANNON: Visitors to the Wilfreds' beautiful new modern home are impressed with evidences of wealth.
Designed by architect Richard Hanna,
It is striking enough in a community of beautiful ranch-type homes to attract half-a-dozen sightseers to the front door daily.

*(Room: SHANNON has crossed to S L entrance; CAROL rises from easy chair.)*

CAROL: And aside from being a beautiful, light, and airy house,
It is a miracle of easy housekeeping, Shannon,
*(Room: she gestures, crosses center.)*
With a complete line of Frigidaire home appliances
For pleasanter living,
For easier living,
For more economical living.

SHANNON: In fact...
*(Room: she catches beachball tossed from S L entrance.)*
Her daily routine is so well planned that Carol spends part of almost every day
At...the beach!
*(Room: she tosses beachball to CAROL.)*

CAROL: Yes! Winter temperatures in Delray average seventy-six degrees,
And in summer,
Gulf Stream breezes keep the mercury at a comfortable eighty.

*(Room:* SHANNON *has crossed down S R of* CAROL.*)*

SHANNON: I hear you're even getting interested in the Garden Club, Carol.

CAROL: That's right!
And you know... *(Sotto)* ...End-O-Pest provides all the pest protection most gardens need against chewing and sucking insects,
And fungus diseases, Shannon.

*(Room:* JASON *enters S L.)*

JASON: Evening, dear...

CAROL: Oh, hello there, dear!

*(Room:* CAROL *tosses beachball to* JASON *who tosses it off S L while crossing to her S R side, as* SHANNON *crosses further S R.)*

CAROL: Dinner'll be ready in just a few minutes—
Meat loaf and chocolate cake—
You and Divina can squabble over the last piece.
*(Room: she puts arms around* JASON's *neck.)*

JASON: Now that's the kind of close-in fighting I really enjoy, honey!
You see before you a man about to sit down to his favorite meal with his favorite family.

*(Room:* CAROL *puts her head on* JASON's *shoulder as* SHANNON *speaks into mike.)*

SHANNON: Yes, just as soon as he can spurt home from work,
Jason's gray-blue convertible is parked outside their watermelon-pink front door,
For the Wilfreds are a spectacularly devoted and home-loving pair....

JASON: Can I give you a hand, dear?

CAROL: Just get everyone rounded up, please, dear—
I'll be right there.
*(Room: she exits S L.)*

SHANNON: A tireless personality with great drive...

JASON: *(Calling)* Divina!

SHANNON: And a range of interests that includes politics...

DIVINA: *(Off)* What?

SHANNON: Photography...

JASON: Dinner-time!

SHANNON: And modern architecture,

*(Room: JASON crosses S R, upstage of SHANNON, to entrance; SHANNON follows behind him.)*

SHANNON: Jason is always delighted for an excuse to be with his family, Although Divina—

JASON: Divina!

SHANNON: A charming and determined young lady...

DIVINA: *(Off)* In a minute, Dad!

SHANNON: Is the squeaky wheel that gets the grease, he says!

*(Room: SHANNON crosses down center as CAROL enters S L with meat tray, crossing to table.)*

JASON: Hmmmmmmmm....
I wonder what's gotten into her?

*(Room: JASON crosses to S R side of table, as CAROL crosses to S R entrance.)*

CAROL: Oh, she just has a lot on her mind, dear, that's all.

JASON: Yes, I'm beginning to think that she has.

CAROL: Divina—your dinner's waiting....

*(Room: CAROL exits S R as JASON crosses to easy chair and sits down. SHANNON at rail, center, on mike.)*

SHANNON: So, this is Delray Beach....

CAROL: *(Off)* Divina?

SHANNON: Not a fashionable resort,
But a small, friendly, forward-going American town,
Concerned with its churches and schools,
Band concerts and football teams—
The best kind of town, the Wilfreds feel,
To be found anywhere in the world.

JASON: Well, that's right, Shannon—
But you know, the defense of the United States is in a condition at which I am appalled.

SHANNON: Ladies and gentlemen, Mr Jason Wilfred.

*(Sound: "Applause" button. Room: SHANNON crosses to easy chair and sits on S L arm, holding mike for JASON to speak into.)*

## Scene Eight

JASON: You see, an article in the current issue of the *Saturday Evening Post*
   has convinced me that if war should break out tomorrow,
We would suffer major initial disasters and be driven back on this continent
   to face a decade or a generation of desperate strife.

SHANNON: That's the current issue of the *Saturday Evening Post*
With the picture of *(Describe cover)* on the cover.

JASON: Of course, we wish to be strong so we can prevent war;
But the *Post* explains how, instead of appearing strong and resolute,
We are continually on the verge of appeasing,
And being alternately irresolute and desperate.
Shannon, no people in history have preserved their freedom
Who thought that by not being strong enough to protect themselves,
They might prove inoffensive to their enemies.

*(Office: lights up as* CLIFF *takes identical magazine from desk drawer, and speaks on mike.)*

CLIFF: That's the *Saturday Evening Post*,
The magazine that hits the heart of America,
And certainly does in this article: "Is America Sleeping?"

JASON: I mean, I'd rather see an adequate radar defense network than a
   television set in every home,
Which seems to be about what we are going to get.

SHANNON: Thank you, Mister Wilfred.
*(Room: she rises, crossing behind chair to extreme S R side of performance space to store mike.)*

JASON: Thank you, Shannon.

CLIFF: And thank you, Shannon Malleson.

*(Sound: crossfade from "Mood 2" to "Tomorrow Tone")*

## Scene Nine

CLIFF: You know, folks,
As the season approaches when the occurrence of poliomyelitis threatens in
   some communities,
And mothers naturally become apprehensive,
We in the Health Department are asked literally hundreds of questions:
Shall I keep Jimmy home from the playground and the movie?

Is swimming dangerous?
In short: How can I protect my child from polio?

*(Room:* JASON *has crossed up to S R wall where he eyes* SHANNON. *This dialog overlaps* CLIFF's.)

JASON: We have no tactical air force worthy of the name, Shannon,
And neither have our allies.
We had better get at it.

CLIFF: Unfortunately, we have to reply
That it is impossible to give answers which will be right for all children in all places.
Most mothers know, however,
That among children who get polio,
Those who have had tonsillectomies within the past few weeks are *twice as likely*
To get the deadly bubar type.
Children with bubar polio are in much greater danger.
So if symptoms appear, call the Health Department at once.
Do not take a child with these symptoms to a doctor's office.
If it is polio, you would thus endanger the others.

*(Room:* JASON *has moved close to* SHANNON *in semi-darkness; his talking stops* CLIFF, *who glowers.)*

JASON: Now, the Russians have forty-thousand tanks, okay?
Many of these are heavy tanks, and among the best tanks in the world, by current measure.
Yet, there has been built and tested ammunition for a gun
Which can penetrate any armor a tank can carry!

*(Sound: add "Jazz Offbeats." Office:* CLIFF *cuts* JASON *off.)*

CLIFF: Only the doctors in your community are in a position to judge
Whether polio virus is present.

JASON: ...light, inexpensive guns,
Which can be used as squad weapons or carried in a Jeep!

CLIFF: So, by keeping in touch with the Health Department,
Mothers need have no great fear
As another polio season approaches.

JASON: Now, when a Jeep can meet a heavy tank and be a match for it, Shannon,
The day of the heavy tank is done.

*(Room:* DIVINA *enters S R, crosses up to* JASON *to give him a kiss, then to up center chair at table, where she sits; as* CAROL *enters behind her S R and crosses to S L chair and sits.)*

## Scene Ten

JASON: Well...good evening!

DIVINA: I'm sorry, Dad.

*(Sound: fade out "Tomorrow Tone." Room:* JASON *crosses to S R chair at table and sits, as* SHANNON *moves to S R rail, on mike, in spot.)*

JASON: That's okay—we can wait—we always do....

SHANNON: Yes, Delray Beach is just a typical town....

JASON: What's gotten into you, young lady?

*(Office: fade lights.)*

SHANNON: Its houses are simple and largely of wood,
Painted white and surrounded by friendly lawns—
Those native shacks burning over there contained literature or guns or large stocks of rice....

*(Room:* JASON *serves as* DIVINA *passes him plates.)*

CAROL: So—did you have a nice day, dear?

DIVINA: Just wonderful, Mom—I mean...it was okay.

JASON: Just wonderful, hunh? Well, that means only one thing.
Who's the young man?

CAROL: Jason...

JASON: Oh, yes, I forgot, Carol—
Your little girl is saving herself for higher things than mere men.

SHANNON: To the right, the main street leads up a hill.
This is the business center.

DIVINA: All I said, Dad,
Was that the starry-eyed attitude about romance is so much schmaltz.

SHANNON: Elegant shops of men's and women's apparel,
Jewelry and leather goods,
Tempt you with their window displays.

CAROL: Could you pass the salt please, dear?...
Thank you.

SHANNON: But after dark, the loudspeakers begin to blare over the rice paddies,
Telling the people not to sell their rice to the government.

JASON: Well—Washington is playing Norton this week.

DIVINA: Don't worry, Dad—we'll wipe the floor with them.

CAROL: Divina, really.

JASON: No, Carol—we've got a fine team, all right.
'Course, the Coach ought to train that Selden Clark for defense as well—
We've got some holes there....

SHANNON: At the first turning stands the Health Department,
One of the most modern in America.
Further down are a school, a nursery, and a recreation center.
But every morning after dawn, patrols work over this road,
Looking for telltale signs of digging.

CAROL: So, I take it the staff meeting of the *News* went well, dear?

DIVINA: Pretty well, Mom.

JASON: Read your piece in the latest issue—not bad.
What's this one about?

DIVINA: Oh, nothing, Dad—real dull stuff.
It wouldn't interest anyone.

SHANNON: There is the inevitable drugstore with its soda fountain.

CAROL: Well, it doesn't sound dull to me, dear.

SHANNON: The movie—yes,
At the first superficial glance,
You wouldn't suspect the uniqueness of this town.
But then you notice the barbed wire fences.
The experiments which are conducted day and night behind those fences
Are America's most effectively guarded secrets.
*(Room: she exits S R, with mike.)*

CAROL: What did you say, dear?

DIVINA: I'm sure I haven't the faintest idea, Mom,
And could I please have the sunporch tonight,
Because Selden Clark is coming over to study.

CAROL: Why, darling—how nice—
Why don't you wear your new black velveteen?

DIVINA: Don't you think that's a little dressy for studying, Mom?
Anyway, I wouldn't have time—
Selden's coming over at seven-thirty.

JASON: Well, now—Selden Clark—
Maybe I could pass on to him some tricks I learned in my football days.

DIVINA: Actually, Mom, would you mind if I didn't finish?
I want to change and brush up a bit.

CAROL: Well, I think you ought to eat something....
Oh, go ahead, dear—
You can raid the refrigerator later....

(*Room:* DIVINA *exits S R Office: lights up,* CLIFF *on mike.*)

CLIFF: As a doctor,
I hear the things a son or daughter won't tell you.

CAROL: Well, I think it's wonderful....

(*Sound: fade "Jazz Offbeats" out slowly.*)

CLIFF: "Aw, gee, Pop—why can't we get a television set?"
You've heard that.

CAROL: Divina's been a—well—you know, so....

CLIFF: But there's more you won't hear.

CAROL: Well, anyway, I think it's very nice.

CLIFF: Do you expect your child to find words for the deep loneliness she's feeling?

JASON: They all seem clean-cut to you.

CLIFF: Do you expect her to blurt out the truth:
That she's ashamed to be with the gang,
Because she doesn't see the television shows they see?

JASON: Your anxiety to become a grandmother is warping your judgment, Carol.

(*Sound: crossfade in "Low Rumble" slowly*)

CLIFF: No, your daughter won't ever tell you the humiliation she's felt in begging those precious hours of television from a neighbor.

JASON: In my opinion, there's something the matter with him.

CLIFF: And yet, you give your child all the sunshine and fresh air and vitamins you can.

CAROL: Why do you say that?

CLIFF: What about sunshine for her morale?

JASON: There's always something the matter with them.

CLIFF: What about vitamins for her mind?

JASON: That's the only kind she's interested in.

CLIFF: Doctors agree—
Television is all that and more for a growing child.

CAROL: She's maternal, that's all.

CLIFF: You see,
Social competence is a big force in any child's life;
And today, it is practically impossible for boys and girls to
"Hold their own" with friends and schoolmates unless television is
    available to them.

JASON: Probably marry some weakling, just so she can mother him.

CAROL: She won't! And, Jason—
You stay out of the sunporch tonight.

CLIFF: So, take it from me—
When television means so much to your child,
Can you deny it to your family any longer?

*(Window: SHANNON leans in at down S R corner, with mike, in spot. Office: fade out lights.)*

SHANNON: Then, across their laughter, tragedy struck!
And revealed in Carol depths of fortitude she never knew existed!
While driving Jason to work one morning
When the roads were slippery with wet leaves,
She skidded and stalled and was hit broadside by another car!
*(Window: she leaps off, S R.)*

CAROL: The car in front of me just seemed to poke along.
Although I am normally a careful driver,
I lost patience, and just as we were approaching a hill,
I took a chance.
As I pulled alongside...

*(Window: SHANNON enters S R, as before.)*

SHANNON: Her own car was demolished, and Carol a broken heap on the
    floor,
With her teeth jarred loose,
All her ribs on one side broken,
And a broken back!

CAROL: The car in front of me just seemed to poke along.
Although I am normally a careful driver...

JASON: Actually, dear, would you mind if I didn't finish either?
I've got some business to attend to myself.

*(Sound: crossfade from "Low Rumble" to "Big Country")*

SHANNON: Then, across their laughter, tragedy struck!
*(Window: she leaps off, S R.)*

JASON: Things are going on in this territory that are suspicious and
    mysterious.

The men keep bringing in reports of wagon tracks—
Three times in the past week, wagon tracks—
But nobody ever sees any wagons.
Well, I intend to get to the bottom of it.
*(Room: he rises and crosses back around chair to window.)*
I'm sending a patrol out to Comanche Territory to look for signs of Indian migrations.

CAROL: Comanche, dear?

JASON: Maybe Comanche, maybe Setank.

CAROL: Setank, dear?

*(Room: JASON puts foot on windowsill at S L edge.)*

JASON: Kiowah chief, honey—big medicine man—
He's worse than Comanch.

CAROL: Well, I've never had a dinner fall apart on me quite this fast before, but
Go ahead, dear—
*(Room: she rises and crosses to JASON.)*
I'll save some chocolate cake for you.

*(Room: CAROL exits S L with two plates JASON holds out his hand in window, and an arm extends from S L side of window with cowboy hat, which he takes and puts on.)*

JASON: And another thing, Carol.
Those two Indian braves in the guardhouse,
Convicted of running guns to the Indians?

CAROL: *(Off)* Yes, dear?
*(Room: she enters S L with tray, clears table.)*

JASON: Send a detail to carry out the sentence of the court.
They're to be executed and their bodies buried outside the post—at once, Carol!

CAROL: Yes, dear.

JASON: This thing's dragged on for months.

*(Room: JASON exits S L; CAROL continues to clear Office: CLIFF exits S L. Sound: crossfade from "Big Country" to "Mood 2")*

## Scene Eleven

CAROL: Goodness—I wish Jason wasn't so fussy.
Always wants his orange juice just squeezed—and he means just!

*(Window:* SHANNON *enters S L with two glasses of orange juice.)*

SHANNON: Have you ever tried serving him Bird's Eye Orange Juice, Carol?
Tastes better than just-squeezed—and takes only forty-five seconds to fix!
Just add cold water and shake—wow!—what juice!

CAROL: Don't tell me this is frozen orange juice?
Tastes better than just squeezed—
Or any frozen juice I *ever* tasted!
Believe me, Shannon—
I'll never be talked into taking anything but Bird's Eye!

SHANNON: And for meal that's good and doesn't take time, Carol—

*(Window:* SHANNON *is handed plate of chicken from S L.)*

SHANNON: Serve Bird's Eye Fried Chicken Paprika!
It's wonderful, and takes less than forty minutes.
You see—Bird's Eye chicken comes ready for the skillet.
*(Window: she holds plate up; chicken is glued on.)*

CAROL: And every bird's a best bird, Shannon—
A plump and juicy young bird!
It's the tastiest chicken I ever sailed into!

SHANNON: Well, you know, Carol,
When I serve Bird's Eye Fried Chicken Paprika at my famous little suppers,
*(Room: she steps over S L windowsill to enter.)*
Celebrities beg me for the recipe!

*(Room:* SHANNON *and* CAROL *squeal with excitement, then sit:* SHANNON *up center,* CAROL *S L, at table.)*

SHANNON: But now, living in Florida as you do,
You also enjoy salad meals all year round, don't you?

CAROL: Well, yes, we do, unh-hunh....

SHANNON: In fact, I understand you have an interesting philosophy about salads.

CAROL: That's right.
We hardly ever have the same salad twice, Shannon.
*(Room: she turns out to audience.)*

*(Out)* Ours is a basic salad, you see, with variations,
Like a basic fashion wardrobe with accessories.

*(Sound: crossfade from "Mood 2" to "Jazz Piano Trills")*

SHANNON: Isn't that interesting?
And how does that work on a daily, uh—

CAROL: Well, Jason and I collaborate on it.
I'm the V P, or Vegetable Preparer, Shannon—
I have everything ready,
And then Jason presides over the dressing and tossing.
I must say, Jason has very definite ideas about salad dressing.

SHANNON: He certainly does, Carol—
But you know, folks, having tried it,
I think Jason has a mighty good idea worth trying in anybody's salad.

CAROL: Well, I'm sure he'd be glad to hear you say so, Shannon.

SHANNON: Well, good...

*(Window:* JASON *as* JIMMY RINGO *enters S L crossing S R; behind him,* CLIFF *enters S L as* DOC.*)*

## Scene Twelve

CLIFF: Ain't you heard?

JASON: Heard what?

CLIFF: Everybody in town's talking about the hold-up.

SHANNON: Of course, greens are the ground work for any tossed salad.

CAROL: That's right.

CLIFF: They figure maybe it was Frank James....

*(Window:* JASON *turns to* CLIFF.*)*

CAROL: I prefer to use romaine and lettuce.

JASON: Did you say Frank James?

CLIFF: That's what they say—
And you can get ten thousand dollars for him,
Dead or alive.

CAROL: And then for variety, I'll add...

JASON: ...Frank James...

CAROL: ...well, in fact, anything I've prepared:
Tomatoes... Sliced cucumbers... Radishes...

JASON: What's he doing around here, Doc?

CLIFF: Comanche Territory's crawling with Indians, Jimmy.
*(Window: he crosses S R to JASON.)*
Supposing his mission is to lead an armed uprising?
All he has to do is gather up a few thousand men and call them soldiers....

CAROL: Slivers of cheese... Cubes of cooked meat... Raw spinach leaves...

*(Window: CLIFF crosses behind JASON up S R.)*

CLIFF: 'Course, Frank James gets blamed for everything.

JASON: You never lived in Comanche Territory, Doc.
You couldn't possibly know the kind of people we had to deal with:
Bushwhackers—murderers—
Frank James shot down women and children in cold blood, Doc.
And I'm going to get that outlaw if it's the last thing I do.
*(Window: he crosses S L.)*

CAROL: Sometimes I'll even add sliced cooked beets to please Jason,
Although I don't care for them myself.

CLIFF: That may take some doing....
*(Window: he crosses down S L to JASON.)*
They say he's away—in Comanche Territory.

JASON: Oh, he's away, all right, you may be assured of that.
But he'll return.
And when he does, I'm going to get him.
Oh, he's got spies everywhere, yes.... but so have I.

*(Window: JASON crosses up behind CLIFF S R; CLIFF turns to follow him.)*

JASON: They tell me he's kind of a natural man.
Say he don't look too different from a lot of fellows.
See, you can tell a snake by his shape and a skunk by his stink, but an
    outlaw...? Well,...
You cain't tell an outlaw by his face,
But he's somebody's next door neighbor.
So you watch for him—listen for him—
Memorize, remember, study every suspicious scrap of talk—
Because you will recognize him, not by his face,
But by the unmistakable odor of his words.

*(Window: DIVINA as MISS PEGGY enters S R crossing up behind JASON.)*

JASON: The stench is un-American!
*(Window: JASON, sensing someone behind him, wheels and draws on PEGGY;
beat, then laughs and tips his hat.)*

## Scene Thirteen

JASON: Miss Peggy...

*(Window:* DIVINA *crosses down to* JASON.*)*

DIVINA: Going hunting, Mister Ringo?

*(Window:* JASON *exits behind* DIVINA, *S R.)*

JASON: Man hunting...

*(Window:* CLIFF *follows* JASON *off S R, behind* DIVINA, *as he exits he twirls his cane.)*

CLIFF: Ma'am...

*(Sound: crossfade from "Jazz Piano Trills" to "Mood 2." Window:* DIVINA *watches men exit, turns and exits S L.)*

## Scene Fourteen

CAROL: *Tuesday*, Shannon, we'll have a big steak or chops with the salad, if the budget's ahead that week, which more than likely it isn't, so I'll do something with hamburgers,
Which we like in all manner of ways....

SHANNON: Unh-hunh...

CAROL: A kind of chile is our favorite.
Wednesday is our casserole day—
Even in hot weather, Jason wants something hot and filling—
I've never been able to get away with serving a salad as the main attraction,
No matter how appetizing and decorated it may be.

SHANNON: Unh-*hunh*...

CAROL: Now, Thursdays are my off-the-record days.

SHANNON: No work.

CAROL: No work.
In the afternoons I take care of a Brownie Girl Scout troop,
Maybe go shopping,
So dinner has to be truly quick and easy that night, Shannon.
*(Out)* Now, to me, this one is it,
And what's more, it satisfies a hungry husband.
I buy the frozen sandwich steaks and take them out of the freezer compartment at noon.

*(Room: CAROL freezes as SHANNON says:)*

SHANNON: When Carol was about ten,
She overheard an adult say:
What a pity she's such a plain child, when her baby sister is so beautiful.

CAROL: We like them on toast with pan gravy.

*(Sound: crossfade from "Mood 2" to "Slow Remorse." Room: CAROL freezes as SHANNON says:)*

SHANNON: After that, Carol understood why,
When she came to her mother with her face streaked with tears,
Her mother would jeer:
You're your father's child—go to him—go away!

CAROL: And I usually have ice cream and chocolate sauce on hand.

*(Sound: add in "Jazz Piano Trills." Room: CAROL freezes as SHANNON says:)*

SHANNON: Her wealthy, spoiled mother would not tolerate anything around her that was not beautiful.

CAROL: The sauce is the real, old-time kind.

*(Room: CAROL freezes as SHANNON says:)*

SHANNON: "She had the money and she called the shots," Carol recalls feelingly;
And she can vividly remember painful scenes over money between her mother and her handsome, West Point father,
From whom she learned the virtues she practices today.

CAROL: They used to serve it hot over ice cream when I was a youngster—
It drips down all over the ice cream and sort-of hardens.
We love it.

*(Room: CAROL freezes as SHANNON rises and says:)*

SHANNON: After that, she was rarely home with her quarreling family.

*(Sound: cut out "Jazz Piano Trills")*

SHANNON: It still hurts to remember, however,
The time she came down with typhoid when her mother was planning a lavish dinner party for her younger sister.
"Oh, Carol," exclaimed her mother, "how tiresome of you.
Go to your room and lock your door."
*(Room: she crosses S L with juice glasses.)*
None of the guests at the gay dinner party that evening
Suspected there was typhoid in the house.

*(Room: SHANNON exits S L. SELDEN as FRANK JAMES enters S R.)*

## Scene Fifteen

SELDEN: You know why I come here, don't you?

CAROL: I guess I do.

SELDEN: How is she?

CAROL: Fine.
*(Room: she rises and continues clearing table.)*

SELDEN: I want to see her, Mrs Kenniston.

CAROL: You think she wants to see you?

SELDEN: Where can I find her?

CAROL: I'm afraid I can't tell you that, Frank.

SELDEN: What do you mean, you can't tell me?

CAROL: All right, then—won't tell you.
*(Room: she exits S L with tray.)*

SELDEN: Why?

CAROL: *(Off)* Because nobody here knows who she is, Frank. She's got another name now, and another life.
*(Room: she enters S L with sponge.)*
And it looks to me like that's the way she wants it to stay.

*(Room:* SELDEN *crosses to S R edge of table.)*

SELDEN: How'd you like to see that street out there full of gunplay?

CAROL: I'd rather not.

SELDEN: Well, that's probably what you'll have in a couple hours.
*(Room: he sits in S R chair at table.)*
'Cause I ain't leaving here till you get a hold of her for me.

CAROL: And what if she don't want to talk to you?

SELDEN: You let her do the decidin' about that.

CAROL: Will you go, then, if I tell her?

SELDEN: Just leave it to her—that's all I ask.

CAROL: I'll see what I can do about it.

*(Room:* CAROL *exits S L with last of table settings. Office: lights up as* CLIFF *enters S L and sits behind desk, looking through file.* JASON *hovers in entrance.)*

## Scene Sixteen

CLIFF: Won't you come in, please, Mr Wilfred?
My name is Doctor Sinclair.
So—you're concerned about your wife?

*(Sound: fade out "Slow Remorse" to silence. Office: JASON enters, crosses down around chair to rail.)*

JASON: Our family doctor gave me your name, Doctor.
And he said, "I don't take cases like Carol's anymore.
But you go and call the Health Department,
And they'll tell you what's wrong and what to do about it."
I hope you don't think I'm always as jumpy as this,
But this is not easy for me, Doctor.

CLIFF: Naturally, these things aren't easy for the families of the patients.
Won't you sit down, Mister Wilfred?

*(Office: JASON sits in patient's chair, S L.)*

JASON: Thank you.

*(Office: CLIFF rises and perches on S L edge of desk.)*

CLIFF: Now, tell me,
How long has it been since you first noticed anything
Peculiar
In your wife's actions?

JASON: Doctor...
Everything I tell you is confidential, isn't it?

*(Blackout)*

*(Sound: "Saint Descent." Room: SELDEN exits. Office: lights reveal CLIFF sitting behind desk, writing in file; JASON in S L chair.)*

## Scene Seventeen

JASON: ...Well, our paths crossed at Saks' one day when she tangled up a sales check—
I made a few sarcastic remarks about her addition,
And she replied she wished she had never left Klein's
Where the customers were all gentlemen.
She was completely spoiled,
But even so we clicked immediately.

She struck me like a small package of dynamite.
That very evening, I asked her to a party,
And seven weeks later we were married.

CLIFF: I see. Please, go on.

JASON: Well, we honeymooned in Maine, visited friends in Vermont,
Moved to New Haven where I got an excellent job with the Bell System doing statistical research....

CLIFF: Yes...

JASON: Then, across our laughter, tragedy struck....

CLIFF: Mmmmmmmmm... Tell me, Mister Wilfred?

*(Sound: slow fade in of "Hymn Drone")*

JASON: Yes, Doctor?

CLIFF: Do you have any trouble at the time of intercourse?

JASON: Why, no, I—don't think so, Doctor....

CLIFF: No pain, or...

JASON: Not particularly...

CLIFF: The experience is satisfactory, you could say?

JASON: Yes.
I think so.

CLIFF: Good.
Please continue, Mister Wilfred.

*(Office: lights fade. Sound: swell "Hymn Drone;" SHANNON on S R mike, off. Window: spot on earth glows brighter.)*

## Scene Eighteen

SHANNON: *(Off)* And now,
Let us turn the clock forward to the Robot Era of 2150.
With peace and reason ruling,
With vast numbers of highly developed robot machines,
And with plenty of atomic and solar energy available,

*(Sound: add "Slow Remorse")*

SHANNON: What would life be like then...?

*(Sound: cut out "Hymn Drone." Window: lights up, DIVINA as MISS PEGGY enters S R crossing up, followed by CAROL as MRS KENNISTON; they both look down S L.)*

## Scene Nineteen

DIVINA: Did you ever see anything so terrible in your life? It's like the whole town's gone crazy.

CAROL: He's here to see you, you know.

DIVINA: Have you seen him?

CAROL: I just left him.
Why don't you see him, if only for a few minutes?

DIVINA: Oh, Mrs Kenniston—what good would it do?
*(Window: she crosses down center.)*
It's over now, you know that.

CAROL: Not for him.
*(Window: she crosses down center, S R of DIVINA.)*
He's still crazy about you, Peggy.

DIVINA: He was crazy about me before, but that didn't stop him from being the kind of person he was.
*(Window: she turns S R to CAROL.)*
He scares me, Mrs Kenniston—he really does.

CAROL: He might have scared you then, but not now.
He's different.

DIVINA: How different?

CAROL: The way Bucky was different that last year. You know—
*(Window: she takes DIVINA's arm.)*
Not wild any more, just sorry.

*(Window: DIVINA turns away from CAROL.)*

DIVINA: And what good did that do Bucky?

CAROL: None, I guess.... But I liked it.

*(Window: DIVINA turns back to CAROL.)*

DIVINA: Oh, if only he'd stayed away!

*(Window: CAROL turns to DIVINA.)*

CAROL: Is it somebody else, Peggy?

DIVINA: No, of course not—you know it's not!

CAROL: Not Jimmy Ringo?

*(Window: DIVINA backs away S L.)*

DIVINA: Jimmy Ringo—why do you ask that?

CAROL: Is it?

DIVINA: I'd never even thought of Jimmy like that.

CAROL: Of course not.
You think he never thought of you like that?

DIVINA: I doubt it... Jimmy's just... Well, Jimmy's just Jimmy.
Oh, really—you must be out of your mind!

*(Window: she turns, crosses S L to corner. CAROL crosses S L behind her.)*

CAROL: Then it's still Frank, isn't it?

DIVINA: I guess so.
I guess it always will be.

*(Window: CAROL, her arm around DIVINA, leads her off S L; SHANNON, with mike, leans in down S R, in spot.)*

## Scene Twenty

SHANNON: *(Out)* Are you always lovely to love?...
Suddenly...breathtakingly...you'll be embraced...kissed...held!
Perhaps tonight.
Be sure then that you are always lovely to love...
Sweet and alluring...
Never uncertain...
Try Stopette,
The deodorant in the amazing squeezeable bottle.
Hello, again, I'm Television Star Shannon Malleson,

*(Sound: "Applause" button covers cut from "Slow Remorse" to "Mood 2." Room: SHANNON enters over S R sill, passing mike back off through window, and crosses center.)*

SHANNON: With a very special message for all you older teens,
Brought to you by Stopette,
The deodorant in the amazing squeezeable bottle.
Because, whether you know it or not,
You've changed a lot, girls—
And now is the time to start taking all that big-gal attention in your stride!
So... When a boy jumps to his feet as you come in the room,
Or holds your drink in a hamburger hangout—
That's a compliment.
And when he makes like a miler to open the car door for you,
That's a compliment, too.
Just remember—

All it takes is a smile from you to make him feel
Able as Gable and
*(Room: she makes a "V" sign.)*
Twice as lucky!

*(Room:* SHANNON *exits S R. Office: lights reveal* CLIFF *sitting at desk,* JASON *in S L chair, his head in his hands.)*

## Scene Twenty-one

JASON: ...then, after weeks in the hospital,
Carol was brought back home in a Bradford brace—
A steel spine,
With claws to catch her shoulders and a belt to go about her middle!
Once in it she was helpless to go out or do anything except barely totter around.

*(Sound: slow fade out of "Mood 2" to silence)*

JASON: When I left in the morning, I would belt her in,
And all day she would sit,
Watching the cars go by,
The pressure of the brace becoming increasingly intolerable until she was in tears of agony when I came home...
For eight months she endured this, Doctor—
Trying to distract her mind from the pain and the loneliness by reading cookbooks—
The basis, no doubt, of her excellent herb cookery today.

CLIFF: I'm sorry, Mister Wilfred—
But in this case it would be a useless gesture to expend the time and talents of valuable therapists when their energies can be directed towards individuals with a more favorable
Rehabilitation Potential classification.

*(Sound: fade in "Telephone Ring" low)*

JASON: Is she in danger, Doctor?

CLIFF: It could be....

*(Room:* DIVINA *enters S L with books, crosses to window.)*

CLIFF: I'll be frank to say I think she's in danger of something.

*(Room:* CAROL *enters S L, watches* DIVINA.*)*

CLIFF: So, we'll make no more guesses until we've had an opportunity to find out, shall we?

*(Sound: slow fade in of "Jazz Off Beats." Office: lights fade. Room: lights up)*

## Scene Twenty-two

CAROL: Your young man is a little late, isn't he, dear?

DIVINA: Mom, for heaven's sake—don't call him "your young man."
*(Room: she sits at table, center.)*
He's only coming over to study.
I wish everybody wouldn't act like we were going steady.

*(Room: CAROL crosses S R behind DIVINA.)*

CAROL: You know, Divina—
When a boy spurns you, or seems to,
It is not necessarily a reflection on you.
It doesn't prove that you're a flop.
You can't click with everyone you meet.
*(Room: she sits at table in S R chair.)*
That would prove you were a malleable clay dummy,
Who pushed and pulled her personality into shape to match everyone else,
Not a flesh-and-blood girl,
With definite ideas of her own.
So if Sheldon or whoever-it-is—

DIVINA: Selden, Mom...

CAROL: Yes, dear.
So if Selden, the boy you think is so wonderful,
Wants to take somebody else to the dance,
It's futile to go over everything you said and did.

DIVINA: Jeepers, Mom—do you mind?
I'm trying to get a little work done!

*(Room: CAROL rises, crosses behind DIVINA's chair.)*

CAROL: Would you like a cookie, dear?

DIVINA: No, thank you, mother.

CAROL: Some chocolate cake?
Studying always made me hungry.

DIVINA: No thanks.

CAROL: There's orange juice.
Some orange juice?

DIVINA: Thank you, mother. That would be very nice.

CAROL: *(Out)* Bird's Eye Frozen Orange Juice!
It's bound to be better!

(Room: CAROL *exits S L;* SHANNON *enters S R, smoking. Sound: cut out "Telephone Ring"*)


### Scene Twenty-three

SHANNON: Of course, poise is a big part, too, of acting your age.
You see, boys like girls who seem at ease because that makes them feel more relaxed, too.
(Room: *She crosses to S R side of table, gives* DIVINA *her cigarette as she takes off gloves, etc.*)
But often, on those big evenings,
When both the date and the dress are new,
Poise can be slow to come....

DIVINA: And how!...
Say, Shannon—what was that formula you were telling everybody about for getting a boy interested in you?

SHANNON: Oh, that...
(Room: *she takes cigarette, puffs, takes a bow off her own hair and ties it around* DIVINA's.)
So why the sudden interest, Divina?
Could it be that you hanker after that Selden Clark?

(Sound: *crossfade from "Jazz Off Beats" to "Hootenanny"*)

DIVINA: Well, I wouldn't put it that way, exactly.
But he is one of the nicest boys I ever met, I will say that.

SHANNON: Oh, he's glamorous, okay—
And he plays football like a dream.
So that's why you've been walking around in a daze lately.
(Room: *she crosses to S R chair and sits.*)

DIVINA: Well, I don't see why you're so surprised.
Ever since he transferred to the High, every other girl in the Senior Class has been—darn it!

SHANNON: But he'd be wonderful for you, Divina.

DIVINA: Well, I wasn't planning on taking him as a tonic.
But I'm glad you approve—
He's coming over tonight.

SHANNON: Over here? Tonight? You minx—what a triumph!

DIVINA: Save your raves for the stag line, Shannon.
He fell all over me in the library this afternoon.
He had Latin to do and so did I—
Then he got snowed under, somewhere around *veni, vidi, vici,*

And anyway, I helped him,
And he's coming over tonight for more.

SHANNON: Well, don't cry about it, for heaven's sake!

*(Room: DIVINA rises.)*

DIVINA: Oh, Shannon—do you think I should have worn my new black velveteen?
Do you think I should mention football to him?
Do you think I have too much lipstick on?

SHANNON: Hey—calm down, Divina—take it from me:
What guys really go for are sweet-smelling Stopette girls.
*(Room: she rises, producing small bottle.)*
You see, I use Stopette myself,
And so I recommend it to all my fans.
Just an effortless squeeze of the Stopette Flexi-Plastic bottle does it all.
And Stopette carries the Good Housekeeping Seal of Approval,
So you know it's safe, as well as effective.
This smaller size—purse or travel size, I call it—
Contains up to six months supply, and sells for just sixty cents plus tax.

DIVINA: But Shannon—
Here I am practically desperate with Selden Clark coming over,

*(Window: SELDEN crosses S R to S R, with books.)*

DIVINA: And all you do is yakkety-yak about Stopette!

SHANNON: Play smart, Divina—
Never risk offending others needlessly.

DIVINA: Gee... Maybe you're right.

*(Room: DIVINA takes the bottle. Sound: "Doorbell" button covers crossfade from "Hootenanny" to "Mood 2.")*

DIVINA: Oh, jeepers—there he is—I've got to run!
*(Room: she crosses S L, then back to SHANNON to give back the bottle, then exits S L.)*

SHANNON: *(Out)* How about you?
Are you sure of your present deodorant?
Ask yourself:
Are you always lovely to love?

*(Sound: SELDEN and DIVINA, offstage, on S R mike. Room: SHANNON exits S R.)*

### Scene Twenty-four

DIVINA: *(Off)* Hiya, Selden...

SELDEN: *(Off)* Oh, hi, Divina...

DIVINA: *(Off)* How are ya?

SELDEN: *(Off)* Yeah... I mean, fine—
How are you?

DIVINA: *(Off)* Oh, okay, I guess....

*(Sound: crossfade from "Mood 2" to "Piano Suspense." Office: lights reveal* CLIFF *sitting behind desk;* JASON *rises from patient's chair and bangs desk.)*

### Scene Twenty-five

JASON: It's no use, Doctor!
I just can't take it any more!

CLIFF: Look, Mister Wilfred—
You don't have to do this, of course,
But if you do, you'll know that you've done everything humanly possible to keep your marriage intact.
If you don't,
You're going to wake up one night and say to yourself:
Maybe this would have made the difference.
Maybe Carol could have become the woman she was when I married her.

*(Office:* JASON *sits down again, S R chair.)*

JASON: Operate, you mean?

CLIFF: That's right—right away.
There's no time to be lost.

JASON: And you can't tell me anything more definite about it?

CLIFF: I'm afraid I cannot.
If the problem is attacked vigorously at this time and properly coordinated,
With first things coming first,
It can be put in satisfactory condition in a few years.
If she drifts as she is going,
It will remain in unsatisfactory condition,
And may well lead to disaster.
Can we reach her by telephone, Mister Wilfred?

*(Sound: slow fade out of "Piano Suspense" to silence)*

JASON: Yes. She's at home now.

CLIFF: Good.
*(Office: he rises.)*
You get her and tell her I'm coming right over.
Don't worry, Mister Wilfred.
You're doing exactly the right thing.

*(Office:* CLIFF *exits S L; fade lights. Room:* SELDEN *enters S L with books,* DIVINA *following;* SELDEN *crosses S R to window corner;* DIVINA *crosses S R to up center chair at table.)*

## Scene Twenty-six

DIVINA: Well, I'm glad you found your way without any trouble.

SELDEN: Yeah—sure was nice of you to let me come, Divina.
I was really in deep trouble this afternoon.
Guess I'm not the Latin type.

DIVINA: Oh, it's not so bad, once you catch on.

*(Room:* SELDEN *crosses down S R to easy chair.)*

SELDEN: *Hic, hac, hoc*—
Why do they make us learn this stuff, anyway?

DIVINA: But don't you feel as if
Your friends, and the books you read, and the music you listen to,
As if they all become a part of you?

SELDEN: Well, yeah, I suppose some people look at it that way,
But football and baseball and so forth,
They're more important to me, I guess.
*(Room: he turns to face* DIVINA.*)*

DIVINA: Guess I just couldn't imagine living without books.

SELDEN: Yeah.
Guess I never thought of it that way, particularly.
I don't get to read too much.

DIVINA: Yeah.

SELDEN: Pretty swell layout you got here.

DIVINA: Yeah, it's nice.

SELDEN: You're kind of bashful, aren't you?

DIVINA: A little.
*(Room: she crosses down to* SELDEN.*)*

DIVINA: Most everybody is, you know.
You're more self-conscious than I am—
That's why you act as forward as you do.

SELDEN: Yeah. So—um,

*(Room: by advancing on DIVINA, SELDEN backs her up S L to table.)*

SELDEN: Are we going to study in here?

DIVINA: Well, sure, if that's okay—
There's a table right over here.

*(Sound: fade in "Fiddle")*

SELDEN: Yeah.
So, where were we?

*(Room: DIVINA slips around table to up center chair, taking S R chair with her around corner and putting it S R of center chair.)*

DIVINA: Right here...

*(Room: DIVINA sits center, opening books as SELDEN crosses and sits in S R chair, opening books. Office: JASON rises from S L chair and crosses far S R at pipe rail, in spot, as: Window: CLIFF, as DOC, enters up S L and crosses S R, leading CAROL as MRS KENNISTON center.)*

## Scene Twenty-seven

JASON: *(Out)* You know Frank James, don't you, Mrs Kenniston?

CAROL: More or less, I guess.

JASON: What do you mean, more or less?
You either know him or you don't.

CAROL: I only know him by sight, Jimmy.

*(Rail: JASON turns up to face CAROL.)*

JASON: But you were there when this thing happened—
Didn't you recognize him?

CAROL: How could I?
They wore masks.

JASON: Yes, we know that they were masked, Mrs Kenniston,
But you could still give us a physical description, couldn't you?

*(Sound: crossfade from "Fiddle" to "Cowboy Train")*

CAROL: Well...he's got two hands, like everybody else...
I'm sorry, Jimmy—
It all happened so fast, and then I got scared and ran.

*(Rail:* JASON *turns out to audience.)*

JASON: The truth of the matter is,
You people are all scared to death of that outlaw.

CAROL: If you were living around here before the war,
You'd be afraid of him too, Jimmy.

JASON: I was here before the war—remember?

CAROL: Then you ought to know what happens to people who turn in an outlaw.

JASON: Mrs Kenniston, this is not Comanche Territory—
This is a law-abiding community,
And we won't have Frank James running wild through our streets,
Shooting and killing our women and children.

CAROL: He ain't exactly running wild through our streets.

JASON: When I want your opinion, Mrs Kenniston, I'll ask for it.
This is an outrage—
Frank James literally running wild through our streets—
*(Rail: he turns back to* CAROL.*)*
Of course, you can't say for sure it was Frank James.

CAROL: That's right.

JASON: In fact, you can't even say for sure that it wasn't.

*(Sound: crossfade from "Cowboy Train" to "Fiddle")*

CAROL: Why, no—no, I can't.

JASON: Well...
Getting you to admit that was quite something.

*(Rail:* JASON *starts to cross back S L in spot. Window:* CLIFF *crosses down to* CAROL *and leads her off, S R.)*

JASON: Thank you, Mrs Kenniston.
That's good enough for me.

*(Office:* JASON *exits S L. Room: lights fade brighter;* SELDEN *&* DIVINA *as before, studying at table, S R and center respectively on upstage side.)*

### Scene Twenty-eight

SELDEN: ...8 and 4 is 12, put down 2 and carry 1...

DIVINA: If you don't mind—
A differential 6 over M to the 30th power...
The half-way check result is:
262 thousand to 341 thousand both using tangent E.
Correct?

SELDEN: Uh....
That isn't the result that I have....

*(Room:* DIVINA *takes* SELDEN's *paper.)*

DIVINA: It must be the same.
I have to say that you've made an error and discard your figures.

*(Sound: add "Slow Boogie-Woogie")*

SELDEN: I didn't make any error.

DIVINA: You made a mistake in your addition.

SELDEN: I did not!
*(Room: he rises and crosses up S R to window corner.)*

DIVINA: There's an error there, Selden—I'm sorry.

SELDEN: Why bother saying you're sorry?

DIVINA: Surely you're not going to let emotion enter into this?

SELDEN: No.

DIVINA: Then we'll continue computing using my results as a basis.

*(Sound: add "Tomorrow Tone." Room:* SELDEN *turns to face* DIVINA.*)*

SELDEN: Hey—why can't you be more like a girl?
Nothing but work, work, work—can't you ever relax?

DIVINA: Oh, and I suppose you think women should only cook and—

*(Room:* SELDEN *sits at table in S R chair and "studies.")*

DIVINA: And, and sew and bear children.

SELDEN: Well, there's such a thing as going overboard in the other direction, too, you know.

*(Office:* SHANNON *enters S L and sits at desk.)*

SELDEN: ...Never suspected you knew so much about everything...

DIVINA: ...At least I'm well mannered....

*(Sound: fade out "Slow Boogie Woogie" and "Fiddle" from "Tomorrow Tone" Office: lights up; SHANNON on mike.)*

## Scene Twenty-nine

SHANNON: Stand by for a special announcement.
At four o'clock this morning,
North Korean armed forces began unprovoked attacks against defense positions of the Republic of Korea
At several points along the 38th Parallel.
Fighting is now in progress along the Parallel.
Both Korean officials and the security forces are handling the situation calmly and with ability.
There is no reason for alarm.
As yet, it cannot be determined whether the northern Communists intend to precipitate all-out warfare.
Mission personnel are advised to travel about as little as necessary.
The Ambassador requests that Mission personnel remain at home or at their posts,
As the situation may dictate.

*(Sound: crossfade from "Tomorrow Tone" to "Jazz Piano Trills")*

SHANNON: Our next announcement will be heard
At three o'clock this afternoon.

*(Office: lights fade; SHANNON exits S L, with mike. Room: JASON enters S L, crossing down S R to easy chair to sit as CAROL enters S L crossing S R to table with plate of cookies; SELDEN rises.)*

## Scene Thirty

JASON: *(Reading)* So...how are things at the Brain Factory?

DIVINA: Just fine, Dad.

CAROL: Are you two making any progress?

SELDEN: Oh, yes, thanks—Divina's a real brain.

DIVINA: Mom—Dad—this is Selden Clark.

*(Room: DIVINA rises; CAROL places cookies S L on table and reaches S R behind DIVINA to shake SELDEN's hand.)*

CAROL: How do you do, Selden?

SELDEN: How do you do, Mrs Wilfred.

*(Sound: add "Telephone Ring")*

JASON: *(Without looking up)* Good evening, Clark.

SELDEN: Good evening, sir.

CAROL: Well, I thought you two might enjoy a snack. Studying always made me hungry....

SELDEN: Me, too—say, these cookies look swell.
*(Room: he crosses S L behind DIVINA to cookies.)*

CAROL: Just help yourself—there's more if you want them, Selden.

*(Room: SELDEN crosses back to S R chair at table.)*

CAROL: And cold fresh orange juice.

DIVINA: Orange juice, Selden?

SELDEN: Oh, yes, thanks.

CAROL: And how about a slice of chocolate cake?

SELDEN: Gee, I'm supposed to be in training, but...
Sure—okay.

*(Room: CAROL exits S L.)*

SELDEN: That's sure nice of your mother, to go to all that trouble.

DIVINA: Oh, Mom loves to cook.
*(Room: she sits at table in center chair, motions to SELDEN to sit again.)*
Besides, have you noticed how bad the meals have been getting in the cafeteria lately?

*(Room: SELDEN sits at table in S R chair.)*

SELDEN: I'll say—they're sure crummy.

CAROL: *(Off)* I'll get it!...

*(Sound: cut out "Telephone Ring")*

SELDEN: All the fellows on the team are complaining about it.

*(Sound: CAROL offstage on S L mike)*

CAROL: *(Off)* Hello?...

DIVINA: You know, Dad used to be quite a football player in his day, too.

CAROL: *(Off)* No, this is her mother....

SELDEN: Yeah, I know.

CAROL: *(Off, not miked)* Divina!

SELDEN: Coach talks about him all the time.

CAROL: *(Off, not miked)* It's for you, dear....

DIVINA: Will you excuse me for a moment, please?

SELDEN: Sure...

*(Room:* DIVINA *exits S L)*

CAROL: *(Off, not miked)* Anyone else for chocolate cake?

*(Room:* JASON *puts down his magazine.)*

JASON: Well...speaking of the team, Selden,
How do you feel about next Saturday?

*(Sound:* DIVINA *offstage on S L mike)*

DIVINA: *(Off)* Hello...?

SELDEN: Oh, okay, I guess, Mister Wilfred...

DIVINA: *(Off)* Listen, Shan—the situation here is critical!

SELDEN: We worked out a couple tricky plays at practice tonight.

DIVINA: *(Off)* We are endeavoring to build up the force necessary to hold the enemy, but to date our efforts against his armor and mechanized forces have been ineffective.

*(Room:* JASON *rises, pacing first slowly S L, then upstage by S L wall of room.)*

DIVINA: Our own troops are fighting with valor under overwhelming odds of more than ten to one,
But the Army is entirely incapable of counteraction,
And there is grave danger of further breakthrough.

*(Sound: crossfade from "Jazz Piano Trills" to "Jazz Offbeats")*

JASON: Right—but I think the backfield is your main worry.

DIVINA: *(Off)* All indications are the situation is disintegrating so rapidly we may not be able to get out.

*(Room:* JASON *crosses S R behind* SELDEN *to window.)*

SELDEN: Well, you could have something there, Mister Wilfred.
But don't you worry about Norton.
They've got a green team—it'll be a cinch.

DIVINA: *(Off)* Was considerable fighting around East Gate and Chongno areas...

JASON: Well, maybe Norton, but...

DIVINA: *(Off)* Resistance combined police and Army...

JASON: ...Ridgefield is something else again.

DIVINA: *(Off)* ...overcome by Wednesday noon.

JASON: Take last Saturday.

DIVINA: *(Off)* All prisoners killed immediately.

JASON: If you'd been playing Ridgefield,
You'd have been sunk on that end play.

*(Sound: add "Tomorrow Tone" to "Jazz Offbeats")*

DIVINA: *(Off)* There is no fighting now in Seoul.

SELDEN: How do you mean?

*(Room:* JASON *crosses behind* SELDEN *to table, center, and draws on* DIVINA's *paper.)*

JASON: Well, look—now this was how the play was set up...
You see...?

DIVINA: *(Off)* All People's Army forces preceded by tanks in every advance;
Enemy soldiers surprisingly young and small compared our Army,
Heavily armed with tommy guns....
Captain Sinh says fight will all be over by this afternoon....

JASON: ...so, you see—
If that pass had gone wild and been intercepted,
You'd have left yourself wide open....
*(Room: he crosses S R behind* SELDEN *and exits S R.)*

DIVINA: *(Off)* In meantime has turned over full authority to Chief Army Staff
and radioed people to remain indoors and calm when tanks arrive.

SELDEN: Say, you're right about that, Mister Wilfred.

DIVINA: *(Off)* He says will stay in Seoul with Army Command to end.

SELDEN: I'll talk to Coach about it first thing in the morning.

DIVINA: *(Off)* He despaired of saving anything...
I made no commitment...

*(Sound: fade out "Jazz Offbeats" from "Tomorrow Tone")*

DIVINA: Yes, I'll let you know, but I'm sure there isn't a chance...
....Goodbye....

*(Window:* JASON *as* JIMMY RINGO *enters S R, crossing S L.)*

## Scene Thirty-one

JASON: You're Miz Kenniston's new hired man, ain't you?

SELDEN: That's right.

JASON: You been coming here a lot.

SELDEN: Well—sick horse.

JASON: How sick?

SELDEN: Well, I don't know....

*(Window:* JASON *crosses back S R.)*

JASON: Say, come to think of it—
That horse don't look too sick at all.

*(Room:* SELDEN *rises crossing S R to face* JASON.*)*

SELDEN: Look, I only work for Miz Kenniston, Mister.

JASON: You sure about that?
I'm thinking maybe Frank James gives you your orders.

SELDEN: Frank James? Who's he?

JASON: How long you lived around here?

SELDEN: Eight months.

*(Sound: slow crossfade from "Tomorrow Tone" to "Low Rumble")*

JASON: Then you're a liar—
Because no man can live in Delray Beach and not know Frank James.

*(Room:* SELDEN *crosses to rail down center.)*

SELDEN: I don't get into town so much.

JASON: You were in town yesterday.
You were in Bergdorff's saloon.

SELDEN: All right.

JASON: You had a beer there with another fellow.

SELDEN: Yeah—old friend of mine.

JASON: Old friend of yours...
*(Window: he crosses S L; puts foot on sill.)*
Now, they took pictures of them outlaws—doggone if one of them didn't look just like that friend of yours....

SELDEN: Naw...Steve Brill?
Why, he works on a farm over in Comanche Territory.
He and I come from the same town.

JASON: Oh, you lived in Comanche Territory before you came here?

SELDEN: That's right—I was born there.
Everybody knows me.
*(Rail: he turns upstage to face JASON.)*
If you don't believe me, why don't you ride on over and ask them?

JASON: Well, maybe I will.
Sorry to have bothered you

*(Window: JASON starts to exit S L as DIVINA as MISS PEGGY starts to enter S R; as, Room: SELDEN starts to cross up to window as CAROL, in nightgown, carrying tray with orange juice, starts to enter S L; Sound: swell "Low Rumble;" All characters freeze as, Room: SHANNON runs on S R crossing center in spot.)*

## Scene Thirty-two

SHANNON: Wrong?!
Yes, they were wrong—but, remember:
They lived in a Time of Violence and an
Age of Strife.
Men and Women Dedicated to what was to become a
Lost Cause.
Some called it War.
But in Delray Beach it was worse than war—
It was neighbor against neighbor with blazing torch,
And lash,
And hangman's rope!

*(Room: SHANNON exits S L. Window: DIVINA moves S L toward JASON.)*

## Scene Thirty-three

DIVINA: Jimmy?

JASON: Why, good evening, Miss Peggy.

DIVINA: Jimmy, what's all this talk we hear that it's Frank James stirring up the Indian with promises that they'll have this land back when the war is over?

*(Room: CAROL crosses to table, sets tray S L.)*

JASON: Well, figure it out for yourself, Miss Peggy.
At any time, Setank could throw a thousand braves against us.
Fortunately, that's not the Kiowah way—
They raid and run.

(*Window:* DIVINA *turns away, S R.*)

DIVINA: Oh, why do you men like to fight?
For hatred? For killing?

JASON: No, ma'am—the war's most particular to me.

(*Window:* JASON *crosses S R to* DIVINA, *behind her. Sound: crossfade "Low Rumble" to "Slow Remorse"*)

JASON: But the war's a long way off—least it seem so round here:
Let's keep it that way, shall we?

CAROL: Orange juice, Selden?

JASON: That's a beautiful dress.

SELDEN: Oh, thanks, Mrs Wilfred.

DIVINA: What makes you say that?

CAROL: Want to pour yourself one?

JASON: I was merely trying to pay you a compliment, Ma'am....
(*Window: he looks back down S L.*)
Yup—real Southwest night...

SELDEN: How long were you going to keep it up?

CAROL: Keep what up?

SELDEN: Keep watching me from the door.

(*Window:* DIVINA *also looks back down S L.*)

DIVINA: "Blemishes are hid by night,
And all our faults forgiven...."

SELDEN: It was making me nervous.

(*Room:* CAROL *crosses center, toward* SELDEN.)

DIVINA: The world should live by night, Jimmy.
Dark draws people together—they can feel the need for each other....

CAROL: You're very attractive when you're nervous, Frank,

(*Window:* DIVINA *crosses S L in front of* JASON.)

DIVINA: But the world gives the night for the sick—keeps for itself daylight—
That lets men look into faces filled with fear and hatred.
Are you filled with fear and hatred, Mister Ringo?

JASON: All the time, Ma'am.

CAROL: Come on—let's dance.

(*Window:* JASON *crosses to* DIVINA *as, Room:* CAROL *crosses to* SELDEN.)

DIVINA: Then you're bound to be a great man one of these days, aren't you?

CAROL: It's been a long time for me.

SELDEN: Say, I ought to go and find Divina, Mrs Wilfred. She kind of wandered off.

(*Office:* CLIFF *as* LIBDER *enters stealthily S L, beckons to* SHANNON *as* HUDRAY *to follow him; they watch the room as, Room:* SELDEN *steps past* CAROL *and crosses up S L to exit until she stops him by saying:*)

CAROL: Don't go!

JASON: You know, you've been a great deal in my thoughts, Miss Peggy, Even when I didn't see you.
They say that thoughts, like time, can't stand still....

(*Room:* CAROL *crosses to* SELDEN; *whispers:*)

CAROL: This was on the arrow:
Blue follows the Green.
The Gray is under the Blue.
The Red is to the right of the Green.
The Gray must go five leagues to the point of 8,
And then return seven leagues to meet the Red.
I want you to know, Frank.
I understand why you are on your guard.

DIVINA: But time can stand very still, Mr Ringo.

(*Room:* CAROL *crosses down S R to easy chair and sits.*)

CAROL: How long are you staying here tonight?

SELDEN: That all depends.

CAROL: Depends on what?

DIVINA: Good night, Mr Ringo.
(*Window: she exits S L.*)

SELDEN: Good night, Mrs Wilfred.

(*Room:* SELDEN *exits S L. Office:* SHANNON *has crossed S R behind desk.*)

## Scene Thirty-four

SHANNON: Beautiful...
The mind that conceived this must have been of a high order of intelligence.

CLIFF: At least the equal of Corplum...
Perhaps considerably above ours.
To think that complex organized society existed here once.

*(Office:* SHANNON *crosses S L to* CLIFF.*)*

SHANNON: Yes, ironic, isn't it?
The mind, wherever you encounter it—Corplum or Poskon—
The highest attainments of the intellect always diverted to self-destruction.
*(Office: she crosses down to rail, S L.)*
What a lesson for our world!
One blast—thousands of years of civilization wiped out!

CLIFF: But there's always the possibility of a meteor.

SHANNON: No, this is definitely blast coupled with extreme heat.
Perhaps the entire surface of the planet is one vast ruin.

CLIFF: Maybe now I can convince you to go back to the ship.

SHANNON: No, we can't stop now—
We must find out what kind of creatures they are!
*(Office: she exits S L.)*

CLIFF: But we don't know how many there are—and supposing they're hostile?
A blast like this—I should hate to think that anyone survived.
We still don't know all the genetic effects of radiation,
But that it will produce mutations, malformations, disfigurements—blindness—
*(Office: he exits S L.)*
*(Off)* That much we're sure of from research!

*(Window:* JASON *turns upstage to his left as* SELDEN *as* FRANK *enters S R crossing up.)*

## Scene Thirty-five

JASON: Listen, stranger—I'll make a deal with you.
You tell me where he is, I'll see you get the money,
Every single dollar of it.

*(Room:* DIVINA *enters S L crossing to table to straighten her books.)*

SELDEN: I don't know what you're talking about.
I never saw Frank James in all my life.

DIVINA: In case you didn't know it, Mother,
You're looking at the social flop of the year!

*(Window:* JASON *crosses S R to* SELDEN.*)*

JASON: You're lying.

*(Room:* DIVINA *runs down S R to easy chair and puts her head in* CAROL's *lap, crying.)*

DIVINA: The first chance he got, he galloped out of here.

SELDEN: You know so much, what are you wasting your time with me for?

DIVINA: Oh, brother, how dumb can a girl get?

SELDEN: Why don't you go out and get him?

JASON: I don't know where he is—I told you that.

DIVINA: She's behind the eightball, and she doesn't even know it.

SELDEN: Well, you won't find him where he was yesterday,
That's for sure.

DIVINA: Do you think I'm happy?

JASON: That I know.

DIVINA: I'm not happy.

*(Sound: crossfade from "Slow Remorse" to "Big Country Short")*

SELDEN: You'll never get him alive, either.

DIVINA: I'm so confused, I—
*(Room: she runs off S R.)*

JASON: Who said anything about getting him alive?
I gave up that idea years ago.

*(Window:* JASON *exits S L. Sound: swell "Big Country Short;"* SHANNON *on S L mike.)*

## Scene Thirty-six

SHANNON: *(Off)* And now, let us turn the clock forward
To the Robot Era of 2150!
With peace and reason ruling—
With vast numbers of robot machines
And with plenty of atomic and solar energy available
What would life be like then?....

*(Window:* SELDEN *[as* FRANK*] turns S R as* DIVINA *[as* MISS PEGGY*] enters S R and runs to him and kisses him. Sound: fade down "Big Country Short." Room:* CAROL *rises from easy chair, crosses slowly up center to table.)*

DIVINA: It's funny—
We've been together such a short time,
And yet it feels like it's been forever.
I don't know....
When we're not together, I—
I feel like I'm suspended in midair,
With nothing down beneath except the end of the world.
I love you so much, Frank.

*(Room:* CAROL *crosses guardedly S L to entrance; stops; then backs away S R to up center chair at table.)*

SELDEN: Your cheek is burning—you're a bundle of nerves.

DIVINA: Don't be my doctor—not tonight—
Just hold me tight—so tight I can't get away from you.

*(Room:* JASON *enters S L crossing S R to table.)*

SELDEN: You're not about to get away from me—
I'll never let you get away.

CAROL: What is it, Jimmy?

JASON: The post is under siege, Mrs Kenniston.

*(Sound: crossfade from "Big Country Short" to "Big Country Long")*

CAROL: Setank?

JASON: Yes, Setank—they've got us surrounded.

CAROL: How many would you say?

JASON: About twelve to fifteen hundred.
But they ain't attacked yet.

CAROL: They never do at night.

*(Room:* CAROL *crosses S L around table to* JASON. JASON *turns away from her, down S R.)*

JASON: Go on—why don't you say what you're thinking?
Say we've got to surrender.
Say there are women and children here.
*(Room: he turns back to* CAROL.*)*
Tell me they're Americans!
Tell me if the post is wiped out it'll be because—

*(Room:* JASON *turns away,* CAROL *reaches to turn him around again,* JASON *kisses her.)*

DIVINA: Oh, Frank, I want to get away from here,
I want to get out of this part of the country,
See if we can't find a little ranch, maybe—
He'll kill you, Frank—I know he will!

SELDEN: But he doesn't even know about us, Peggy.

*(Room:* JASON *drops to his knees in front of* CAROL.*)*

JASON: I'm sorry, Mrs Kenniston

SELDEN: I tell you he doesn't even suspect!

JASON: Better get down and get some feed, Ma'am,
That's about all I can think of for the present.

*(Room:* CAROL *kneels down next to* JASON. *Sound: crossfade from "Big Country Long" to "Big Country Short" and swell.)*

SELDEN: You don't have to worry about me, Peggy.
I can take care of myself.

*(Room:* CAROL *lies on floor and pulls* JASON *down on her.)*

JASON: I've told the men to carry on their assignments....

DIVINA: And what about me, Frank?

JASON: Patch up as best they can...

DIVINA: Every time your man leaves the house, you wonder when he's coming back.

JASON: In a way, I don't suppose it matters....

DIVINA: Every time there's a knock on the door, your heart stops!

JASON: You know what we're in for in the morning.

*(Room:* CAROL *rolls over on top of* JASON.*)*

DIVINA: Every time you pick up the paper, you're afraid.

SELDEN: Peggy, stop it!

JASON: Try and keep it from the children if you can.

DIVINA: You're afraid you'll find he's dead!

*(Window:* DIVINA *runs off S R;* SELDEN *starts to follow.)*

## Scene Thirty-seven

CAROL: *(To* JASON*)* No, wait, Frank—leave her alone!

*(Window:* SELDEN *stops, turns momentarily, then exits S R.)*

CAROL: I didn't want any of these people to get hurt.
They've been good to me, Frank—
Especially Jimmy Ringo and the girl!
They mustn't be hurt, no matter, Frank—do you understand?

*(Room:* JASON *throws* CAROL *off him.)*

CAROL: Why do you think I've been protecting you—covering up for you—lying for you?
I didn't know what I was getting involved in when I saw the hold-up!
Then I found out you were involved and I kept quiet!
But not any more—
I'm through covering up—
I'm gonna identify you, Frank!

*(Room:* CAROL *embraces* JASON; *he pushes her away.)*

JASON: Oh, my god, Carol—you don't even know what you're saying—you don't even know what you're saying—
You're so desperately sick!

CAROL: You are!

*(Room:* JASON *gets up and backs away up S R.)*

JASON: No—you are—you, Carol! All the symptoms!
I didn't marry a woman: I married a mental disease!

*(Sound: cut out "Big Country Short" and fade in "Planets." Room:* CLIFF *enters S L, crossing to* CAROL *as: Office:* SHANNON *enters S L with mike.)*

SHANNON: *(On mike)* Ruptured?...

CLIFF: My name is Doctor Sinclair, Mrs Wilfred.

SHANNON: ...Get relief this proven way...

CLIFF: I'm with the Health Department and I'm here to help.

SHANNON: Get back to normal living with this new appliance innovation that lets you

Run, play, work, lift, stoop or squat,
Like any normal person.

*(Room:* CAROL *gets up and crosses to* CLIFF.*)*

SHANNON: No leg straps, no elastics, no plastics...

CAROL: Then you heard.

SHANNON: ...Flex-O-Pad...

CAROL: Why pretend you hadn't heard?

SHANNON: ...Entirely different...

CAROL: That television, what they said over that television it was...

SHANNON: And a degree of comfort you never thought possible.

CLIFF: Is that what your husband was trying to tell me, Mrs Wilfred?

*(Room:* CLIFF *leads* CAROL *S R to easy chair where she sits; as* JASON *crosses S L behind table and sits in chair at center.)*

SHANNON: Light...inexpensive...guaranteed...

CAROL: Of course he was trying to tell you!

SHANNON: ...Delay may be serious...

CAROL: Do you think he's the only man who ever found me attractive?

*(Room:* CLIFF *shakes a small bottle of serum and fills a syringe.)*

SHANNON: ...Order today...

CAROL: Mr Jason Wilfred doesn't have any feelings!

JASON: No, I have feelings, Carol.
I have pity.

CAROL: Pity!
Nobody pities me!
Nobody pities me, nobody! Nobody!

*(Room:* CLIFF *injects* CAROL *as* JASON *pours a glass of juice. Sound: slow crossfade from "Planets" to "Tomorrow Tone")*

CLIFF: Easy, Mrs Wilfred, easy...
This will make you feel better.

*(Room:* CAROL *sinks back in easy chair as* CLIFF *turns upstage and crosses to window corner, back to audience.)*

## Scene Thirty-eight

CAROL: That night the weather moved in and clouds came down and it began to pour....
I wanted to get to Delray Beach.
But word came that it had fallen into enemy hands.
Through the window, I could see nothing but swirling gray clouds and moisture slipping like soft jewels against the glass.
Two hours out...

CLIFF: Did you make it clear to her that we suspected her of passing information on to Setank?

CAROL: ...the clouds suddenly began to break up....

JASON: Yes.

CAROL: And we could see the roads below us,
Black with people headed south.
Then trains appeared—crawling along a single track....

CLIFF: And what was her reaction?

CAROL: ...all headed south and covered with people.

JASON: ...She seemed surprised and said:
I do not think so.

CAROL: After we landed at Delray,
Something caught my eye in the sunlight.

(*Room:* CLIFF *turns and crosses to S R edge of table, leaning on it with both hands.*)

CAROL: The leading edge of the wing was in flames.
The rubber encasing the de-icer was burning and spurting little orange curls of flame.
The plane seemed doomed....

CLIFF: Did you make it clear to her that we were in possession of precise information on this matter?

CAROL: ...so I waited for her to explode....

JASON: ...Yes.

CAROL: ...but she didn't—
At least, not right away.

CLIFF: ...And what did she say to that?

CAROL: And except for the little orange flames and some smoke curling up from the pilot's window,
Everything seemed quiet.

JASON: She again said: I do not think so.
Perhaps you will tell me what the evidence is.

*(Room: CLIFF crosses S L behind JASON and around S L edge of table, to pour himself a glass of juice.)*

CAROL: By this time, it was getting along toward sunset, and we could see the fire inside glowing brighter, when all at once,
The cabin fire burned through the windows and up through the astrodome and gushed into the cockpit, and the nose burned off, and then the great tail flukes rose slowly against the evening sky as the right wing tanks exploded....

CLIFF: ...And this remained her attitude?

JASON: Yes...

CAROL: ...And even as that beautiful old plane died,
The evening sky turned from old rose to blood red,

*(Room: CLIFF sits down in S L chair at table.)*

CAROL: And flares ignited by the blast fell through the belly of the ship and lay burning on the runway,
Their greens and scarlets reflected by the glistening undersurface of the wings.
Through it all...

JASON: ...I don't know who's the guiltier

*(Sound: swell "Tomorrow Tone" and add "Kiss Drum")*

CAROL: ...as soft umbrellas of flame opened around the plane...

JASON: ...The one who commits the crime;
Or the one who just stands by and does nothing about it.

CAROL: ...other fires began to burn....

CLIFF: ...Sometimes I sit around for hours trying to figure that one out.

CAROL: And tiny stars of incredible intensity showered out of the inferno and lay shimmering and dancing around the ship....
As died the fire...

JASON: ...I mean,
Here we are looking for a bunch of outlaws....

CAROL: ...So died the sunset....

JASON: And when we find them, who will they be?

CAROL: ...And it was cool and dark....

JASON: ...Probably friends of ours...

CAROL: And night lay upon the land

CLIFF: Complicated, isn't it?

*(Blackout)*

*(Room: as lights fade,* CLIFF *crosses down S R to* CAROL *in easy chair.* CAROL, CLIFF *and* JASON *exit in blackout. Window: earthglow reveals* SELDEN *as* FRANK JAMES *at S L corner loading pistol. Sound:* SHANNON *on S R mike)*

## Scene Thirty-nine

SHANNON: *(Off)* And now...
Let us turn the clock forward to the Robot Era of 2150,
And see what life would be like then....

*(Sound: cut out "Tomorrow Tone" leaving "Kiss Drum" to swell. Window:* SHANNON *enters S R with mike in spot.)*

SHANNON: Good evening, sir.

SELDEN: Ma'am.

SHANNON: Mighty windy country.

SELDEN: This ain't even a breeze.

SHANNON: Pretty hot.

SELDEN: Wait till summer.

SHANNON: Really?

SELDEN: If we live that long.

SHANNON: And how much time do you think you have left?

SELDEN: Oh, we're all right as long as them smoke signals is there.
It's when they stop that I'm going to sweat.

SHANNON: Well, cheer up—look—there's more smoke over there.

SELDEN: Oh, this ain't going to be no picayune affair, Ma'am.
Looks like Setank's rounding up the whole tribe.
And that dust there now—
There's a war party underneath that just as soon as you're born.
Don't strain your eyes, Ma'am—
They'll be there tomorrow.
If I know these Indians,

And I ought to,
We're going to see a lot of them before too long.

SHANNON: And what are you going to do about it?

SELDEN: Well, a man who knows this country might be able to bust through if he could get by their patrols—
After dark, of course—
'Course, they're just waiting for us to try it—
That's why they got the patrols out there.
And they can afford to lose a few men—we can't.

SHANNON: But you know this country—couldn't you make it?

SELDEN: Not with a woman tagging along.
I tell you,
I don't mind the sniping, but I sure could do with a lot less of them drums!

*(Sound: cut out "Kiss Drum," reveal "Indian Raid")*

SELDEN: You reckon them buzzards left something around here?

SHANNON: Looks a little like they don't believe you're leaving.

SELDEN: Never did like them things studding on me.
'Taint because the buzzards know what they're doing.
But it brings to mind the question:
Do I know what I'm doing?

SHANNON: And your name again is...?

SELDEN: Oh, I'm a stranger here, myself, Ma'am....
*(Window: he crosses S L, stops, turns back to her.)*
I'm a long way from home, and I can't afford to make any mistakes.

*(Window: SHANNON exits S R.)*

SELDEN: I think nobody has been so far from home as me.

*(Office: in darkness, CLIFF enters S L and sits behind desk; CAROL in bathrobe enters S L and sits in patient's chair, S L. She puts S L mike in stand. Sound: SHANNON on S R mike)*

## Scene Forty

SHANNON: *(Off)* Take a good look at this man....
If you saw him fishing at a summer resort,
Would you be able to tell what he does for a living the rest of the year?
Is he a letter-carrier?

*(Window: SELDEN exits S L.)*

SHANNON: A movie talent-scout?
A tugboat captain?
What would you do if he turned to you and said:

ALL: *(Off)* What's...My...Line?

*(Sound: cut from "Indian Raid" to "Clip Clop." Room: SHANNON enters S R with mike in spot, crosses center.)*

SHANNON: From C B S Studio 51,
Hughes-Farady Incorporated, makers of Stopette deodorant,
The deodorant in the amazing squeezeable bottle,
Brings you television's sensational new game:
What's My Line?
Once again tonight, we're going to put our cameras close up on a few
    people from some varied and perhaps unexpected occupations,
And to start things rolling,
It's time to meet our first challenger—
So won't you come in, sir, and sign in please!

*(Sound: cut out "Clip Clop;" fade in "Planets." Room: fade out spot. Office: lights reveal CLIFF and CAROL.)*

### Scene Forty-one

CAROL: I've been bleeding.

CLIFF: Badly?

CAROL: No, I wouldn't say badly. Just a little...

CLIFF: I see.

CAROL: Every day.

CLIFF: Um-hmmmm...
Then the flow is profuse, you would say.

CAROL: Well, I don't know.

CLIFF: I see.
Tell me, Mrs Wilfred,
Have you had any pain along with this bleeding?

CAROL: No, not very much.
I'm just a little sore and sensitive.

CLIFF: Look, Mrs Wilfred—don't hold out on me—
I was able to feel it plainly during my examination:
A soft boggy mass about the size of a plum,

And extremely sensitive,
As you well know.

CAROL: Yes, it hurt terribly.

CLIFF: And I was as gentle as possible, Mrs Wilfred;
Because I've known such a mass to rupture during just such an examination.
You see,
If the material is allowed to stay inside and rot away,
The inflammation set up by all that rotting process going on in there seals everything tight.
Mrs Wilfred—I believe it's due to rupture in the near future.

CAROL: What happens then?

CLIFF: It's about as bad as can be, Mrs Wilfred.

CAROL: Do you make people happy, Doctor?

*(Room: DIVINA enters S R, crossing S L and up to window corner.)*

CLIFF: I suppose so.

CAROL: Do you make them very happy?

CLIFF: Well, I try to.

CAROL: Do you make them happy with what you do with things—
With instruments, with tools, with—uh—
Or with some nefarious, uh...

*(Rail: spot up on SHANNON as, Sound: buzzer covers cut from "Planets" to "Tomorrow Tone.")*

SHANNON: No, I'm sorry—one down and nine to go—Miss Kilgallen!

*(Office. fade out light. Room: lights up as SELDEN enters S L; fade out spot.)*

## Scene Forty-two

SELDEN: Divina?...
Say—what are you doing in here?
I've been looking all over for you.

*(Room: SELDEN crosses to S L edge of table as DIVINA crosses to S R edge.)*

DIVINA: Oh, I just figured I better lay low until you and Dad settled the football situation.

SELDEN: Yeah, your Dad is a regular guy.
And boy, is your mother a super cook!

DIVINA: Oh, when we go overboard, we really go overboard in this family.
The all-out Wilfreds, we're known as.

SELDEN: You're kidding, of course.
Well—guess I'll have to be traveling along—
Nice evening, Divina.
Sure glad I came over.

*(Room:* DIVINA *crosses center along downstage edge of table.)*

DIVINA: Are you, Selden?
I'm glad, too.

SELDEN: Yeah.
And thanks a lot for helping me.

DIVINA: That's all right, Selden, I—
I enjoyed helping you.

SELDEN: Yeah.
*(Room: he crosses to* DIVINA.*)*
I'm just sorry we never had any time to...

DIVINA: What?

SELDEN: Aw, nothing...

DIVINA: I didn't invite you over to make an incompleted pass, Selden.
I hope I haven't upset you.

SELDEN: What makes you think I blame you for anything?

DIVINA: But maybe I am to blame.
I tried so hard to fight against what I feel—
I didn't want you to know, ever!
You've been so...nice to me, but that's your nature.
It doesn't mean anything.

SELDEN: No, it means something.

DIVINA: Don't look so unhappy, Selden.
Don't worry about me.
I suppose no one ever...died of a broken heart....

*(Room: they kiss; spot up on* SHANNON *at rail as, Sound: buzzer covers cut from "Tomorrow Tone" to "Planets.")*

SHANNON: Two down and eight to go—Mr Untermyer!

*(Room: fade lights as, Office: lights reveal* CLIFF *standing behind desk,* CAROL *in patient's chair, S L.)*

### Scene Forty-three

CAROL: You mean it's going to grow into a cancer?

CLIFF: No, Mrs Wilfred,
But its blood supply could be interfered with,
And it could break down and make you pretty sick,
And even if it didn't do that but just continued to grow,
It might become so large that it could interfere with other important internal organs—
It just grows like grass, Mrs Wilfred!

CAROL: And how...big could it get to be, Doctor?

CLIFF: The largest one I ever removed weighed fourteen pounds;
But I once saw one operated that weighed thirty-three—
You were a foolish woman—criminally foolish—
If you couldn't afford private medical attention, there are clinics!
You never would have got away with it in this town.

CAROL: How did you know it wasn't here that it happened?

CLIFF: Because it would have had to be reported to the Health Department,
And we follow up on such cases.

*(Office: CAROL bangs desk, leaps out of chair and turns off, S L.)*

CAROL: I don't see what business it is of the Health Department!

*(Office: CLIFF sits behind desk.)*

CLIFF: We make it our business, Mrs Wilfred—
And it is a good thing, too—
For the protection of others as well as the one involved.
All you managed to do was let yourself in for years of trouble.

*(Rail: spot up on SHANNON)*

SHANNON: Now, I think it's only fair, Panel, so that you won't be misled,
To say that "No" would be the proper answer to that,
So it's three down and seven to go—Miss Francis!

*(Rail: fade out spot. Office: CAROL turns back to desk.)*

CAROL: But I'm so frightened, Doctor.

CLIFF: Good—
Now, we'll just have to make some preparations....

*(Office: fade out lights. Room: lights reveal DIVINA struggling in SELDEN's embrace.)*

## Scene Forty-four

DIVINA: No...wait a minute!

SELDEN: Hey—what's happening?

DIVINA: No, Selden—stop it—let go of me!

SELDEN: Quit making such a big thing out of it—you ain't hurt!
*(Room: embracing* DIVINA, *he pushes her S R.)*

DIVINA: This is no good, Selden—it's just a sex attraction!

SELDEN: You're right—and name me something better!
You faker—don't you know what you really want?
Well, make up your mind, and make it up now,
Because I'm a restless guy!

*(Room:* SELDEN *kisses her; she breaks away.)*

DIVINA: Let's get something straight.
It'll save us both a lot of trouble in case we should ever run into each other again,
Which I promise you I shall try and avoid!
I think you're a stupid, vicious ape!

*(Sound: slow crossfade from "Planets" to "Low Rumble")*

DIVINA: Now, get out of my way!

SELDEN: You hadn't ought to talk to me like that, you know.
You hadn't ought to.
A girl ought to be friendly to a big football player.
You're just afraid to put out!

DIVINA: I'm just afraid of getting stuck with an ape like you.

SELDEN: You wouldn't mind that, you know—
They say that what the mother goes for,
The daughter goes for, too.

*(Room:* SELDEN *crosses to* DIVINA, *kisses her roughly, throws her to the floor and exits S L, taking his books off table.* DIVINA *runs off S R. Rail; spot up on* SHANNON. *Office: lights reveal* CLIFF *with microphone at rail, S R side of office;* CAROL *in S L chair.)*

## Scene Forty-five

SHANNON: No, I'm sorry, Panel; but I'm going to flip over all the cards,
And let our challenger tell you just exactly what it is that he does....

(*Room:* SHANNON *exits up S R; spot out.*)

CLIFF: (*On mike*) Did you know Frank James as an outlaw?

CAROL: I couldn't be able to say definitely.
I assumed that he was, but I didn't know.

(*Sound: crossfade "Low Rumble" to "Piano Suspense"*)

CLIFF: Did you accept Peggy as an outlaw?

CAROL: I accepted Peggy as a friend.

CLIFF: Jimmy Ringo has testified that Frank James and Peggy were outlaws!

CAROL: I consider that slander and false.

CLIFF: Jimmy Ringo has testified about a meeting
In which Frank James passed information through Peggy on to Setank—
Do you recall such a meeting?

CAROL: There was never such a meeting—I deny it categorically.
I declare it is false!

CLIFF: Have you ever conspired or attempted to transmit
Any secret information from any source to Setank?

CAROL: I have not.

(*Office:* CLIFF *crosses up to S R edge of desk; he places mike in stand at S R edge and leans over it.*)

CLIFF: Was Frank James at that meeting?

CAROL: I will answer no more questions about that meeting.

CLIFF: Was Peggy there?

CAROL: I have refused to answer.

CLIFF: Was your daughter there?

CAROL: The same answer.
You can't infer that any person was or was not there!

CLIFF: Do you know Frank James?

CAROL: I have refused to answer.

CLIFF: Selden Clark?

CAROL: The same answer.

CLIFF: Your daughter?

CAROL: The same answer.

CLIFF: You refuse to say whether you know your own daughter?!

(Sound: crossfade "Piano Suspense" to "Low Rumble")

CAROL: I refuse because it would be helping in a fishing expedition.
Experience has taught me about fishing expeditions such as these.

(Office: CLIFF crosses S L to CAROL.)

CLIFF: Are any of these people outlaws or outlaw sympathizers?

(Office: CLIFF puts CAROL on mike.)

CAROL: I think I'd like to talk to my family doctor, Dr Sinclair.

CLIFF: Do, Mrs Wilfred!
I'll get him on the phone and explain what I've found,
And then let you talk to him....

(Office: CLIFF exits S L; fade lights. Room: DIVINA as MISS PEGGY enters S R crossing S L to center, followed by JASON as JIMMY RINGO.)

## Scene Forty-six

JASON: What you do outside is your own business,
But this is our home!
How could you do this to us?
Am I to believe that you had so little regard for our feelings,
Or for principle,
Or for memory?

DIVINA: Are you completely blind to yourself, Dad?

JASON: I suppose you intend to explain that remark?

DIVINA: With all your talk of purity and honor,
Don't you really know what you want?
If you were only open and honest, it would be less horrible.
You make me feel unclean!

(Room: JASON draws his gun.)

JASON: All right, up with your hands!

DIVINA: Have you lost your mind?

(Room: DIVINA walks S R past JASON, turning him around; JASON gestures with gun, then puts it away.)

JASON: You're an outlaw, ain't you?
Well, I'm taking you prisoner!

*(Sound: add "Indian Raid" to "Low Rumble" and swell. Room:* SELDEN *as* FRANK, *wearing a poncho that conceals his hands, enters S L and crosses down S L.)*

JASON: You will confine yourself to quarters pending further orders.

SELDEN: You're not going to hold a white woman here in the face of an Indian attack, are you, Mr Ringo?

*(Room:* JASON *holds his hands up.)*

JASON: Miss Peggy's safety is my responsibility, stranger.

SELDEN: Miss Peggy is my fiancée, Mr Ringo.

*(Room:* JASON *turns to face* SELDEN.*)*

SELDEN: And there's another thing you ought to know:
Those two Indian braves you shot were Setank's sons—
He doesn't want the rest of us—
It's your scalp he's after!

JASON: What's your real name, boy?

*(Room:* JASON *and* SELDEN *square off.)*

SELDEN: He's closing in on all sides, Pop—
That doesn't matter anymore.

JASON: It matters to me—you're Frank James, ain't you?

SELDEN: That's right—you heard of me?

JASON: Yeah, I heard about you, you miserable outlaw.
I heard you're a cheap, no good, barroom loafer!
And now I'm going to stand you up and shoot you.

*(Room:* DIVINA *crosses S L to* SELDEN, *embracing him.)*

DIVINA: I never wanted it to end this way, Frank.

SELDEN: There never was any other way, Peggy—
We just put it off a while....

DIVINA: Oh, Frank...

JASON: Stand clear, Miss Peggy, or I'll have to shoot you too!

*(Room: with left hand* SELDEN *moves* DIVINA *up S L.)*

SELDEN: You mean, you'd shoot an unarmed woman down in cold blood, Pop?

JASON: You're asking for trouble, son.

*(Room:* SELDEN *holds out right hand, under poncho.)*

SELDEN: And you already got it, Mister—
'Cause I got a gun on you and it's pointed smack at your belly!

(Room: SELDEN *crosses slowly S R towards* JASON. DIVINA *crosses against upstage wall to center. Sound:* CLIFF *speaks from off S R mike.*)

CLIFF: *(Off)* Mrs Wilfred...?

JASON: I ought to blow your head off for laying for me like that!

CAROL: *(On S L desk mike)* Yes, Doctor?

SELDEN: These new .45's really put a hole in a man, Jimmy—
Now, you gonna clear out of here or not?

CLIFF: *(Off)* Why don't you unburden your mind and clear your conscience by telling us the full story?

(Room: JASON *raises both hands.*)

JASON: If I didn't have something else on my mind,
I'd take them guns away from you and slap you cross-eyed!

CAROL: *(On mike)* Yes. Yes, why don't I...
After all...

SELDEN: Why don't I just stroke you one across the snout!

(Room: SELDEN *pulls back poncho to reveal he's been bluffing with a bare hand. Both men drop into gunfighter's crouch and back away. Their challenges overlap with* CAROL's *confession in office, over S L desk mike.*)

## Scene Forty-seven

| CAROL: | JASON: |
|---|---|
| I was engaged in espionage from the middle of 1942 until about a year ago. There was a continuous passing of information relating to atomic energy at irregular but frequent meetings. This illegal association commenced at my own initiative, and no approach had been made to me. I myself spoke to an intermediary who arranged the first interview. This | Are you prepared to back up that remark or not? |
| | SELDEN: How'd you like to try and make me? |
| | JASON: I want to know what you meant by |

was in a private house, where I met a man whom I believed to be Russian. This was early in 1942. After this first meeting, there were two or three meetings for about six months before I went to Delray Beach in December, 1943. The talks were sometimes certainly with Russians, but others were with persons of unknown nationalities. There was a prearranged rendezvous and recognition signals were exchanged. Generally the meetings were of short duration, and consisted of my passing documentary information, and with the other party arranging the next rendezvous. At times I was questioned, but I thought it to have been inspired from some other quarter than my contact. I realized that I was carrying my life in my hands, but I had done this from the time of my underground days in Germany. I said I still believed in Communism, but not as practiced in Russia today.

that remark you just passed.

SELDEN:
Why don't you button up your britches and go home?

JASON:
I'm warning you, Frank—I'm going to get you!

SELDEN:
Yeah, I know—I heard that one before, too.

JASON:
I won't just try it, I'll do it! I got my mind made up, now!

SELDEN:
Then quit talking about it, Mister, and go for your guns!

*(Offstage: string of firecrackers explodes stage:* JASON *and* SELDEN *fall down;* DIVINA *hides under table. Office:* CAROL *rises and exits S L. Window:* CLIFF *as* LIBDER *enters S R, speaking into "instrument;"* SHANNON *as* HUDRAY *enters S L.)*

## Scene Forty-eight

CLIFF: Poskon calling Corplum!
Poskon calling Corplum!
Come in, Corplum, over—
Come in, Corplum!
Can't contact them—they won't answer!

SHANNON: Of course they will—everything will be all right!
We must report everything—tell them as much as we can!

CLIFF: No—it's hopeless—we're lost—everything's lost!
Now Corplum will never know the terrible truths that we learned!

*(Offstage: second string of firecrackers explodes. Room: JASON and SELDEN, who have struggled to their feet, fall down again. Window: CLIFF is hit by gunfire; falls.)*

CLIFF: Murdering savages!

SHANNON: No, Libder—they are crazed, despairing wretches!
Pity them! Pity them!
*(Window: SHANNON takes "instrument" from CLIFF.)*
Poskon calling Corplum!
Poskon calling Corplum!
Come in, Corplum, over—
Come in, Corplum

*(Offstage: third string of firecrackers explodes. Window: SHANNON is hit by gunfire. Room: JASON and SELDEN, who have struggled to their feet, fall down again. Fade to blackout)*

*(Sound: crossfade from "Indian Raid" and "Low Rumble" to "Mood 2." Room: spot on DIVINA, as she crawls out from under table and crosses down center to rail.)*

## Scene Forty-nine

DIVINA: One moment they were all around us, and we were drowning in
    Indians;
Then suddenly, it was over with,
And we had the desert to ourselves.

*(Room: JASON exits S R, SELDEN exits S L. Window: CLIFF and SHANNON exit.)*

DIVINA: So we just ran—
Past the station and over the bridge between the boundaries and the
    railroad tracks,
While the light changed from gray to pale green then back to gold,

Over the ascending monolith of General Hospital,
Leaving the ugly industrial section,
Past endless honey and olive and french-fried almond stands,
Past the acrid smell of dairies and the white silt of quarries,
Past Mexican restaurants with their promise of hot tamales,
Past Moorish motels with their promise of hot nights,
And at our left, canceling out all the ugliness.
Those incredible papier-mache mountains,
Their dawn-stained peaks gradually reddening while the round metal ball of the morning sun moved gradually up from behind like a disk spewed forth from some gigantic blast furnace—

*(Rail: DIVINA crosses S R, as, Room: lights up; CAROL in bathrobe enters S L and crosses center behind table as, Office: JASON enters S L, crosses S R behind desk to watch CAROL; then CLIFF enters S L.)*

DIVINA: Miles and miles and miles of this—
Until we entered the Robot Era of 2150,
Where almost every morning, winter or summer,
Jason and Carol Wilfred waken to sunlight streaming through the pale-gray and aqua bedroom
Of their Delray Beach, Florida, home....

*(Room: DIVINA exits S R. Office: JASON turns to CLIFF.)*

JASON: Is she going to be all right?

CLIFF: I don't know, Mister Wilfred.
She's hurt pretty bad.

*(Sound: crossfade "Mood 2" to "Slow Remorse." Room: CAROL straightens table and chairs.)*

CAROL: *(Out)* ...happened to see Europe again was...
...that trip to the end is coming here tomorrow after the packages arrived...
...yesterday brought good cheer as...
...after my release, I was asked to help Professor R E Peierels on some war work...

*(Office: JASON crosses around desk down S L.)*

CLIFF: I guess she had nothing left to live for....

CAROL: *(Out)* I accepted it without knowing what the work was,
But I doubt if it would have made any difference to my subsequent actions if I had.

JASON: But didn't she give you any explanation at all?

CAROL: *(Out)* You see, if you believe in Sackoy,
You are a good person.

CLIFF: What explanation could she give that you don't already know?

*(Office:* CLIFF *exits S L. Window:* SELDEN *as* FRANK *and* DIVINA *as* MISS PEGGY *enter S L, crossing S R.)*

DIVINA: One battle, and there's so much work to be done.

SELDEN: Yes, but look at them—
Already they're starting to rebuild.

CAROL: *(Out)* In the course of this work, I naturally began to form bonds of personal friendship,
And I had to conceal them from my own thoughts.
I used my Marxian philosophy to conceal my thoughts in two separate compartments....

DIVINA: Is it true what the courier said:
That the war will soon be over?

SELDEN: Yes.

DIVINA: Doesn't the end of the war have to be a beginning?

CAROL: *(Out)* Some people don't like Sackoy,
But I could be free and easy with other people, because they don't like to be punished,
And I knew the other compartment would step in if I reached a danger point.

SELDEN: *Mejores mañanas passaran.*

CAROL: *(Out)* Looking back on it now,
I would call it controlled schizophrenia.

DIVINA: What does that mean?

SELDEN: It means: It'll all seem better tomorrow.

DIVINA: Tomorrow...

*(Window:* DIVINA *and* SELDEN *cross S R to exit. Office:* JASON *exits S L.)*

DIVINA: ...Sure does have a pretty sound....

CAROL: Go—it will be pleasant for you when I am near the table in the dining room was crowded with people it crashed into were screaming that they had been—
You see,
I still believed that Russia would build a new world,
And that I would take part in it.
The earth would be a vast garden.
National boundaries would be obsolete, and language barriers a thing of the past.
*(Room: she crosses down S R to rail.)*

There would be no threats of war.
Hospitals and prisons would be almost empty.
Trips to the moon would be commonplace;
And the crowded cities of today would have disappeared—
In their place, communities planned for better living:
Men and machines together doing the work and play of the world,
Reaching toward an ever-greater harmony,
And orderliness,
And beauty....

*(Room:* CLIFF *as* LIBDER *and* SHANNON *as* HUDRAY *enter S L;* SHANNON *crosses very slowly down S R to* CAROL, *who turns to face her; then* SHANNON *slowly backs up S L again.)*

## Scene Fifty

CLIFF: Whatever you dream, believe the opposite....

SHANNON: Dreams go by opposites....

CLIFF: If you dream of a funeral or a death...

SHANNON: It is a sure sign of a wedding...

CLIFF: If you dream of a marriage...

SHANNON: It is a sign of death...

CLIFF: If you dream of the dead...

SHANNON: You will hear from the living...

CLIFF: If you dream of a flower...

SHANNON: It is a sign of death.

CLIFF: If you dream of a snake, you have an enemy.

SHANNON: If you dream of a fire, you have an enemy.

CLIFF: To dream of a snake that you do not kill
Is a sign that you have an active enemy.

SHANNON: Dream a thing three times,
And the dream will come true.

*(Room:* CAROL *crosses slowly up left toward* CLIFF *and* SHANNON.*)*

BOTH: If a person starts to say something to you and then forgets what he is going to say...

SHANNON: It is a lie.

BOTH: If your shoe comes untied someone is thinking...

CLIFF: About you.

BOTH: If you go to sleep with the moon on your face you will...

SHANNON: Go insane.

(Room: SHANNON *and* CLIFF *turn up S L as* CAROL *walks past them and exits up S L.*)

SHANNON: When a child walks backwards...

CLIFF: It is cursing its parents.

*(Slow fade to blackout)*

END OF PLAY

*New York City*
*20 June 1985*

# THE CRAZY PLAYS

THE CRAZY PLAYS were commissioned by BACA Downtown (Greta Gunderson, Executive Director) with funds provided by the Rockefeller Foundation New American Plays program; and first produced on 8 March 1990, in the BACA Downtown Fringe Series. The cast and creative contributors were:

> Zivia Flomenhaft
> Gary McCleery
> Nicky Paraiso
> Liz Schofield
> Mary Shultz

*Director* .................................................. Jeffrey M Jones
*Score* ................................................... Dan Moses Schreier
*Scenery* ....................................................Kyle Chepulis
*Lights* ........................................................ Pat Dignan
*Costumes* ...................................................Claudia Brown
*Assistant director* ............................................... Jessie Allen

An abridged form of THE CRAZY PLAYS was also presented 21 & 22 April 1990, as part of the Downtown/Uptown Festival at the Manhattan Theater Club.

Since character is not equivalent to identity in these plays—which is to say that all actors play several characters, some of which are also portrayed by several actors—I have chosen in the text to use the names of the original cast members to designate who is speaking. Furthermore, whenever scenes juxtapose two independent lines of action—which is to say, whenever two scenes are intercut—the dialog in the second scene is indented in the text. Finally, it may prove helpful for the reader to have the following schematic diagram of scenic areas referred to in the stage directions:

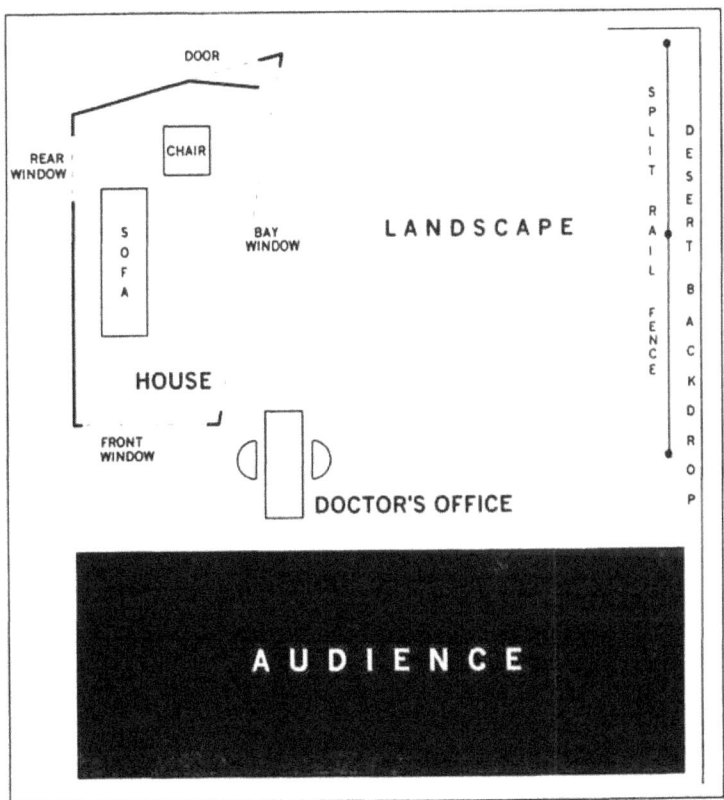

In addition to the songs indicated in the text, a continuous multi-channel tape-loop score has been constructed for THE CRAZY PLAYS which, in the event of production, the authors consider joined to the text.

# CRAZY PLAY #35

# PLEASE HELP ME I'M FALLING

## ACT ONE

*(In the house:* GARY *&* LIZ *on sofa,* NICKY *in chair;* ZIVIA *in doctor's office;* GARY *crosses down to front window.)*

GARY: People say I'm a bad man.
That ain't right.

I ain't no bad man, I'm just doing what I gotta do.
I'm just doing what I gotta do, that's all.
I'm just doing what I gotta do and I ain't no bad man.

Ain't no worse than anybody else and that's the truth.
Ain't no worse than you...

*(*MARY *looks in through rear window as lights fade out.)*

GARY: Think about it.
I ain't no worse than you.

## ACT TWO

*(In the house:* GARY *&* LIZ *on sofa,* NICKY *in chair)*

                LIZ: G'night, hon...

GARY: Goddamn it...

NICKY: What?

                LIZ: Come back real soon...

GARY: Knock it off, son...

NICKY: Dad, I'm not doing anything.

GARY: I'm going to bop you.

NICKY: But Dad, I'm not doing anything!

GARY: Do you want me to bop you, goddammit?

LIZ: G'night, hon...

GARY: Is that what you want?

LIZ: Come back real soon...

NICKY: Dad—what am I doing?
Hunh?

GARY: You know what you're doing.

LIZ: Y'all come back...
Come back real soon now, hon...

NICKY: Then tell me.

GARY: You know perfectly well what you're doing because you're doing it just to bug me!

NICKY: Then why don't you go ahead and tell me?

GARY: Okay, son...

NICKY: You can't—you know why, Dad?

GARY: Have it your own goddamn way...

NICKY: Because I'm not doing anything, Dad.
I'm not doing anything at all....

LIZ: It has been
Our pleasure
To serve you.

GARY: Goddammit...

NICKY: I'm not doing anything, Dad.

LIZ: G'night hon...
Y'all come back...

GARY: Didn't I say, knock it off?

NICKY: Knock what off, Dad?

GARY: Son, I am going to bop you,
I swear to God, I am going to bop you so hard.

NICKY: You better not!

GARY: Then knock it off!

LIZ: G'night, hon...
Y'all come back...

NICKY: You better not bop me!

LIZ: Come back real soon, now, hon...
Y'all come back...

GARY: Son...

NICKY: You better not...

                        LIZ: It has been
                        Our pleasure
                        To serve you.

GARY: Goddamn it...

NICKY: What?

                        LIZ: Sweet home

GARY: Knock it off, son...

NICKY: Dad, I'm not doing anything.

                        LIZ: Sweet home sweet home

GARY: I'm going to bop you.

NICKY: But Dad, I'm not doing anything!

GARY: Do you want me to bop you, goddammit?
Is that what you want?

                        LIZ: Headed home sweet home sweet home
                        You're headed home
                        G'night, hon...

NICKY: Dad—what am I doing?
Hunh?

GARY: You know what you're doing.

NICKY: Then tell me.

GARY: You know perfectly well what you're doing because you're doing it just to bug me!

NICKY: Then why don't you go ahead and tell me?

                        LIZ: It has been....

GARY: Okay, son...

                        LIZ: Our pleasure...

NICKY: You can't—you know why, Dad?

GARY: Have it your own goddamn way...

                        LIZ: To serve you...
                        Home sweet home

NICKY: Because I'm not doing anything, Dad.
I'm not doing anything at all....

LIZ: To serve
To serve
It has been our pleasure
To serve
To serve
G'night, hon...

GARY: Goddammit...

NICKY: I'm not doing anything, Dad.

*(Fade out)*


## ACT THREE

*(In the house: LIZ and GARY on sofa, NICKY stands to one side, looking at them.)*

NICKY: Misfortunes never come singly....
*(He crosses down to bay window talking to audience.)*
Since starting we have always had a regular examination of gums and legs on Sunday, and at first it seemed to show us in a very satisfactory condition.
But tonight Dad told me Mom had angry-looking gums.

LIZ: Not your mom, son.

NICKY: He says there is nothing yet to be alarmed about,
But we have decided not to tell Mom for the present.

LIZ: Not your mom.

NICKY: Instead, we increased the seal allowance.
*(He crosses upstage behind sofa.)*
To Mom this was presented as a preventive measure,
But I am not sure she does not smell a rat.

LIZ: Not your mom, son.

NICKY: You are so.

GARY: Son, she's not your mom.

*(NICKY crosses downstage of the sofa; MARY looks in from rear window.)*

NICKY: Six weeks ago we were very much inclined to swear at the cook, who had been careless enough to leave blubber in our seal meat,
But now we are only too eager to discover that our "whack" has a streak of yellow running through the dark flesh.
Dad examined us again.
I asked him quietly the result.
There is no doubt that Mom is seriously ill.

GARY: She's not your mom.

LIZ: Not your mom.

NICKY: This is a black night...
But things must look blacker yet before we decide to turn.

*(Fade out)*

# ACT FOUR

*(In the house:* GARY *and* LIZ *on sofa;* NICKY *in bay window)*

NICKY: January 16:
The sledges have been running easily,
Gums seem a trifle better....

GARY: (Sheesh—this upset stomach's really getting to me....)

NICKY: The double ration of seal seems to have had a good effect.

GARY: (I feel...terrible, this gas pain is—Whoa!—) (Really making me nauseous—)

NICKY: I could not have believed I should ever have enjoyed blubber this much—
On the other hand—

GARY: (Musta been something I ate...)

NICKY: Under the dark and gloomy sky we stumble frequently,
And this sort of thing is very bad for Mom.

LIZ: Not your mom.

NICKY: Mom...

GARY: Son—she's not your mom.

NICKY: Yes, she is, Dad.

GARY: No, son, she isn't.

NICKY: Dad—I oughta know my own mom!

GARY: No, son, I oughta know, 'cause I'm the doctor.

NICKY: You're not the doctor, Dad!

LIZ: Don't talk that way to the doctor, son.

NICKY: He's not the doctor, Mom.

LIZ: I'm not yer mom.

*(*NICKY *tries to ignore them;* MARY *looks in from rear window.)*

NICKY: This morning Mom woke up with very angry looking gums.

LIZ: Not your mom.

NICKY: We make her do a little pulling....
But twice she slipped down a deep crack and fell,
Coughing and spitting up blood,
And we had to stop for several minutes to watch.

GARY: (Sure wish I could just lie down for a second...)

NICKY: It looks as if life for the next week or two is not going to be pleasant for any of us and it is rather curious...

GARY: (Hoo boy—I don't *know*—what the hell did I eat...?)

NICKY: Because we always looked forward to this part of the journey....

(GARY *collapses on floor in front of sofa.*)

LIZ: G'night, hon...
Y'all come back...

(*Fade out*)

## ACT FIVE

(*In the house:* GARY *on sofa,* MARY *in chair,* NICKY *in bay window*)

MARY: Sweet home, sweet home...
Sweet home, sweet home...
G'night, hon...

NICKY: January 19:

MARY: It has been our pleasure to serve you.

NICKY: Another long "blind" march:

MARY: G'night, hon...

NICKY: Very depressing, and the gloom doesn't tend to enliven our spirits;
We have to carry Mom....

GARY: She is not your mom.

MARY: Listen to the doctor, son.

NICKY: We have to carry Mom on the sledge and at night she spends hours in violent coughing and fitful sleep....

GARY: Pay attention, pay attention to me, boy!

NICKY: If she could only sleep...

MARY: Why don't you listen to the doctor, son?

NICKY: But he's not the Doctor, mom.

GARY: And she's not your mother, son.

NICKY: Yes, she is, Dad—and you're no doctor.
Could I get a second opinion on this?

(ZIVIA *enters house.*)

ZIVIA: Oh, hi, I'm Doctor Scott, Monica Scott.
Uh, did somebody need a second opinion?

NICKY: Yeah, me—
Is this my dad or is this the doctor?

(ZIVIA *crosses to* GARY *on sofa.*)

ZIVIA: Oh, my god.

NICKY: What?

ZIVIA: Oh, my god.

NICKY: What's the matter?

GARY: (Oh, gimme a break!)

ZIVIA: This man was claiming to be a doctor?
This man has no medical training—this man is a patient.

NICKY: See, Mom.

ZIVIA: This man just had a heart attack!

MARY: Not your mom, son.

(ZIVIA *crosses behind sofa.*)

ZIVIA: And she's not your mother, either, so cut it out.

NICKY: What do you mean—she is so my mother!

MARY: No, son—your mom's the doctor.

GARY: (Get him!)

ZIVIA: That's right, son—you're with the doctor, now. (Get him there!)
Just lie down, son, just lie right down there, hold him down there gonna
    give him a hypo—

(ZIVIA *produces a very large syringe; everyone advances on* NICKY, *who collapses on floor.*)

NICKY: Noooooooooooooooooo...

ZIVIA: Son, lemme give you a hypo full of that real...

ALL THREE: ...Good stuff.

(*Fade out*)

## ACT SIX

*(In the house:* GARY *in bay window,* MARY *in chair; in the landscape,* NICKY *upstage center, watching)*

MARY: Had him in a chokehold...

GARY: Oh, they're tough, those guys are tough.

MARY: And the other guy was working on his kidney with a nightstick.
The guy is screaming something—
So they both start jumping on his head and kicking him,
And everybody's just standing around...

*(*GARY *crosses to* MARY, *he puts foot up on chair and she touches his trouser cuff.)*

GARY: Here, feel...

MARY: Nice.

GARY: Nine ninety-nine, marked down—got it on special.
The very last one...
Because when you said pain wasn't going to be the problem....

MARY: Well maybe pain was not the right word...

GARY: But you said pain wasn't going to be a problem, Doc.

*(*MARY, *slipping out of chair, crosses dowstage in the house as* LIZ *enters downstage right, crossing in the landscape.)*

                        NICKY: Captain?

                        LIZ: Yes, Little Bob?

GARY: Doc, please tell me what the problem's gonna be?

                        NICKY: How many of the rabbits died?

GARY: I don't want to die, Doc.

                        LIZ: All of them died, Little Bob.

*(*GARY *follows* MARY *around the house.)*

MARY: Naked boy or naked girl?

GARY: I don't know....
It was sunset,
We were up in the foothills,
And I was alone by the pool except for maybe one or two people over on the deck...

                        NICKY: Did all of them die?

MARY: Where's everybody else?
Back in the house?

>LIZ: They all died.

GARY: No, the house is empty.
The house is very still because whoever lives there is dying of cancer.
Whoever lives there is sitting on the sofa with his wife and the nurse—the Jamaican nurse—who's doing one of those crossword puzzle books.

(NICKY *crosses down center to* LIZ.)

>NICKY: But did they all die, Captain?
>Did all of the rabbits die?

GARY: Weeks?

MARY: Maybe. Maybe weeks.

GARY: A month?

MARY: Maybe a month.

GARY: Six weeks?

>NICKY: Captain?

MARY: Skip it.

(LIZ *crosses upstage center.*)

>LIZ: Every last one.

GARY: I'm in the mood for skip it.

MARY: I've got skip it.

>NICKY: That's very sad.

GARY: I'll get by as long as I've got skip it.

MARY: I can't give you anything but skip it.

GARY: I know a woman way over town she's skip it.

>NICKY: Not even one?
>LIZ: Not even one.

MARY: I cried a river over skip it.

>NICKY: That's very sad.

(LIZ *exits upstage behind house; in the house:* GARY *has cornered* MARY.)

GARY: I want a gal just like the gal that married dear old skip it.

MARY: See, when you say "treatment"...

GARY: But no treatment at all, none at all—I mean I just can't believe that.

MARY: Well, technically speaking there are procedures but....

GARY: What?

MARY: Well, I'm afraid they'd only be a waste of time....

GARY: Boy, I sure could use some medication right now.

MARY: Yeah, me too.
Sure wish I had some of that medication I had yesterday...

GARY: Yeah—what was that stuff?

MARY: Oh, I don't know—just the standard stuff....

GARY: Was that the standard medication,
Or was that some kind of special order?

MARY: No, just the standard...

GARY: Yeah, well, lay it on me...

(ZIVIA *enters the house;* GARY *crosses to her.*)

ZIVIA: You guys need medication?

MARY: You just hit the nail right on the head there, sister.

ZIVIA: You guys sure look like you could stand for a little medicating.
Hunh?
How about it?

GARY: Yeah—matter of fact we were just sitting around talking about our need for medication...

MARY: It's a big need, too.

ZIVIA: Yeah, well, maybe I could help you guys out.

GARY: Yeah...

MARY: Yeah, well, maybe you could...

ZIVIA: Yeah, maybe...
*(She crosses to sofa and sits.)*
What's in it for me though, guys?

(*In the house,* MARY *slips out the door as* GARY *crosses to* ZIVIA; *as* NICKY, *beside the desk, talks to the audience.*)

                      NICKY: We are so fortunate to live in this great nation.

ZIVIA: What's in it for me?

                      NICKY: This is still the land of opportunity.

ZIVIA: What's in it for me?

NICKY: Ours is the best country in the world.
Ours is the best system of government ever invented.
We are the lamp of freedom.
The arsenal of democracy.
We are a good people.

ZIVIA: What's in it for me?

NICKY: And personally, I personally believe in God,
And I believe that God has blessed this land and its people
And for this bounty I give thanks
And I am humbled
And in my heart I know
We will endure.
We shall prevail.
Thank you—
And may God bless and keep each and every one of you.

*(Fade out)*

## ACT SEVEN

*(In the house: LIZ and GARY on sofa)*

GARY: Don't fucking gimme that shit.

LIZ: Listen asshole, you fucking blew it.

GARY: Fuck you.

LIZ: Fuck you, you lying motherfuck.
You're dead meat—you understand?

GARY: Hey fuck you blow it out your ass.

LIZ: You understand?

GARY: Eat shit.

LIZ: Dead fucking meat.

GARY: Peckerhead.

LIZ: Who you calling peckerhead?

*(NICKY enters the house, but stands by the door.)*

NICKY: Hi, Dad.

GARY: Hello, son.

NICKY: Hi, Mom.

LIZ: Hello, darling....

GARY: Better sit down and put your head between your knees, son.
(*He crosses up to* NICKY.)

LIZ: Your father and I have something terrible to say to you, dear.

NICKY: Gee, but it's great to be back home...

GARY: Come here—don't shy away from me.

NICKY: Even though I guess I've been a disappointment to you....

LIZ: Don't shy away from your father.

GARY: I'm not going to hurt you, son.

LIZ: He wouldn't hurt you, honey.

NICKY: Are you going to hurt me, Dad?
Dad...
You're hurting me, Dad...

GARY: Don't be ridiculous, son—this doesn't hurt....

(GARY *leads* NICKY *downstage.*)

NICKY: Dad—it really hurts, Dad!

LIZ: Don't be silly, dear...

GARY: Come here—don't shy away from me!

NICKY: Mom—I feel sick, Mom.

LIZ: Don't be a stick in the mud, dear.

GARY: Come here, boy.

LIZ: You'd better listen when your father speaks to you that way, dear.

NICKY: But it hurts, Mom.

GARY: Hold him down, dear.

NICKY: Mom—help me, Mom!

LIZ: But we're trying to, dear.

GARY: Hold him, damn it!

LIZ: Well, I am trying to, dear,
But your son is biting me.

NICKY: Mmmmoooooooommmmmmmmmm...

(LIZ *pushes* NICKY *on floor as* MARY *appears in upstage house window.*)

MARY: G'night, hon...

LIZ: You're biting me, you bad bad dog.

MARY: Come back real soon...
G'night, hon...

LIZ: Bad dog!

MARY: Back real soon...

LIZ: You bad bad dog!

MARY: 'Night hon, back real soon...
It has been our pleasure to serve you.

*(Blackout)*

## ACT EIGHT

*(In the house, MARY in the rear window on phone; in the landscape, GARY and ZIVIA as cowboys; NICKY upstage center, watching.)*

                        MARY: Can I please just talk to you?

ZIVIA: Four...

GARY: Three...

ZIVIA: Two...

GARY: One...

BOTH: Boom!

                        MARY: Well, maybe I do...

BOTH: Boom!

                        MARY: Cause I need to, okay?
                        Cause I'm trying to understand things.

ZIVIA: Four...

GARY: Three...

BOTH: Boom...

                        MARY: Would you please just talk to me?

GARY: Four...

ZIVIA: Three...

GARY: Two...

BOTH: Boom.

MARY: Listen, if I thought it would help, I'd
say it a hundred times.

BOTH: Boom.

MARY: But I said I'm sorry.

BOTH: Boom.

MARY: Just don't hang up.
Please—don't hang up.

(NICKY *crosses downstage center to desk, as* MARY *and* ZIVIA *exit.*)

NICKY: You know the other day
When I was driving in my luxury automobile,
I said to myself: I really like this automobile.
I like the quiet ride, the smooth and elegant handling—
The caress of leather...
I guess what I'm saying is:
I'm the kind of guy that can appreciate
Attention to detail.
And I said to myself: This is class.
And I said to myself: Damn, I'm good.
And when I looked around me on the freeway I saw people just like me in luxury automobiles.
And I said to myself: This is the good life.
Yeah, it's the good life.
Hey, isn't this the good life, babe?
Yeah, come on and get it.
You know what you want and you want it all.
Yeah—go for it, guy.
You can get it if you really want it.
You just gotta try.

(LIZ, *entering landscape downstage right, crosses to* NICKY.)

LIZ: (Here, doggie...)

NICKY: We are so fortunate to live in this great nation.

LIZ: (Here, doggie-doggie-doggie...)

NICKY: This is still the land of opportunity.

LIZ: (Here, doggie-doggie-doggie, come to momma!)

NICKY: Ours is the best country in the world.
And personally, I personally believe in ruff, and I believe that ruff has ruff-ruff-ruff and...

LIZ: Where's that doggie?

(LIZ *approaches* NICKY, *carrying a stick; he gets down on all fours.*)

NICKY: Ruff-ruff-ruff-ruff!

LIZ: Oh, where's that good dog?

NICKY: Ruff-ruff-ruff!

LIZ: Well, well, well, well—what kind of doggie is this?

NICKY: Ruff-ruff!

LIZ: It's a bad dog!

NICKY: Ro!

LIZ: It's a bad bad doggie!

NICKY: Ro!

LIZ: Time for Mister Sticky!

NICKY: Ro! Rease ron't reat ree!

LIZ: Now, where's Mister Sticky?

NICKY: Ro—rease ron't reet ree, rudder rear!

LIZ: What's that my bad dog says?

NICKY: Rudder, rudder, rease ron't reet ree!

LIZ: I can't hear that bad bad doggie!

NICKY: Relp me! Relp me!

LIZ: Here's Mister Sticky—

NICKY: Rumbuddy relp me!

LIZ: Here comes Mister Sticky!

NICKY: (Jesus, what a twisted bitch!)

(NICKY *stands and confronts* LIZ, *who turns away upstage.*)

NICKY: All right, Mother dear—go on and take a poke—
Come on, take a swing, Mom—I know you love it!

LIZ: Young man, I don't know what you're talking about.
I had merely set out to find my little doggie lost and strayed...

NICKY: Ya mean yer pooch?
Ya mean yer mutt, yer hairy mutt?
(What's the matter—don't you love me, mother dear?)

LIZ: Such a nice little sweet little good little doggie...

NICKY: (Sheesh—what an embarrassment...)

LIZ: Here, doggie, doggie, doggie...

NICKY: (Hoo, boy!)

LIZ: Here, doggie, doggie, doggie—come to mommy's stick!

NICKY: Hey, you...

LIZ: Yeah?

(LIZ *exits upstage behind the house with* NICKY *following; they enter the house,* GARY *watching them from the fence.*)

GARY: People say I'm a bad man. That ain't right.
I ain't no bad man.
Ain't no worse than you. Think about it.
I ain't no worse than you.

(MARY *appears in rear window, singing.* GARY *crosses from fence to house, entering at end of scene.*)

MARY: Johnny was a dead beat
Down on Meat Street
Every time he caught the heat
They put it on his rap sheet

Had a bad brain
Pack it up with Novocain
Start to feel pain
Shoot it up again

Johnny!—Oh, Johnny...

Johnny had a shotgun
Took it on a milk run
When he started having fun
Ya hadda call him number one

Got a fast car
Didn't get far
Got a big scar
Gonna be a star

Johnny!—Oh, Johnny
Oh, Johnny!—Oh, Johnny
Oh, Johnny...

(*Fade lights*)

END OF PLAY

# CRAZY PLAY #30

# HOW A COWBOY SAYS GOODBYE

## ACT ONE

*(In the landscape, GARY and LIZ as cowboys; in the doctor's office, NICKY and MARY enter; She puts a control device on the desk; they watch the cowboys.)*

GARY: Well...

*(Pause; MARY pushes a buzzer on the control device.)*

GARY: So long...

LIZ: So long, Tex...

*(Neither cowboy moves.)*

*(Fade out)*

## ACT TWO

*(In the landscape, GARY and LIZ as cowboys; in the doctor's office, NICKY and MARY watch the cowboys.)*

GARY: Well...

*(MARY pushes a buzzer on the control device.)*

LIZ: So long...

    NICKY: (Wally?)

    MARY: (Shush!)

GARY: So long, Tex...

    NICKY: (This is boring, Wally....)

*(Neither cowboy moves.)*

*(Fade out)*

## ACT THREE

*(In the landscape,* GARY *and* LIZ *as cowboys, In the doctor's office,* NICKY *and* MARY *watch the cowboys.)*

    MARY: (I don't know—
    Maybe it's supposed to be boring.)

    NICKY: (Wally, nothing's supposed to be
        boring.)

    MARY: (Well, I kinda like it.)

GARY: Well...

    NICKY: (You would.)

    MARY: (Shush!)

*(*MARY *pushes a buzzer on the control device.)*

LIZ: So long...

    NICKY: (Don't shush me.)
    (Hey, where do you get off with this
        "shush" crap, anyway?)
    (Man, you are really pushing it!)
    (You can't tell me to shush!)

LIZ: So long Tex...

    NICKY: (I have as much right to be here
        as you do!)

*(Neither cowboy moves.)*

*(Fade out)*

## ACT FOUR

*(In the landscape,* GARY *and* LIZ *as cowboys; in the doctor's office,* NICKY *and* MARY *watch the cowboys.)*

GARY: Well...

LIZ: Yup...

    NICKY: *(Hey, Wally...)*

GARY: Time to hit the dusty trail, Tex.

    NICKY: *(Let's make 'em go crazy!)*

GARY: Well...

LIZ: Yup...

                  NICKY: (Come on...)

                  MARY: (No way.)

                  NICKY: (Why not?)

GARY: Well...

                  NICKY: (Hunh?)

                  MARY: (Because!)

LIZ: Yup...

                  NICKY: (Because you're chicken!)

                  MARY: (I am not.)

GARY: Well...

LIZ: Yup...

GARY: Yup...

LIZ: Yup...

GARY: Well...

LIZ: Yup...

GARY: Yup...

                  NICKY: (Chicken)

GARY: Well...

                  MARY: (Okay, but just this once!)

(MARY *turns the "crazy" dial up all the way;* GARY *leaps center stage.*)

GARY: Yaaaa-hooo!
Yes sir I aim to saddle up my ridey horse 'n' head out 'n' ride it 'n' ride it 'n' ride it 'n' rope it 'n' ride it 'n' shoot-shoot-shoot it 'n' bang-bang-bang ya-hoo yup out on that western plain!
Yaaaa-hoooo a-singin cow-cow yicky-yicky yay yicky-yay
Yaaaa-hoooo a-singin cow-cow yicky-yicky yay.

(LIZ *leaps center stage.*)

LIZ: Yaaaa-hooo a-singin cow-cow yicky cow-cow yicky-yicky
Cow-cow yicky-yicky cow yicky cow yicky cow yicky cow
Yaaaaaaaaaaaaaaaaaaa-hoo!
A singin cow-cow yicky-yicky yay.

                  MARY: Okay—and that's all!

(MARY *turns crazy dial back down;* LIZ *and* GARY *walk back to fence.*)

GARY: Yup.
Well...

LIZ: So long, Tex.

    NICKY: (You're still a chicken.)

GARY: Well...

    MARY: (I am not.)

    NICKY: (You are so.)

LIZ: Yup.

GARY: So long, Tex.

    MARY: (I don't care, anyway...)

GARY: Well...

LIZ: Yup...

GARY: Yup...

LIZ: Yup...

GARY: Yup...

LIZ: Yup...

GARY: Yup...

LIZ: Yup...

GARY: Yup...

    NICKY: (Oh, boy—is this boring and stupid, or what?)

    MARY: Oh-oh...

LIZ: A singin cow-cow yicky-yicky mumbledypeg and skeezix.

(GARY *falls down dead.*)

    MARY: Now look what you did, Gary!!

    NICKY: What?

    MARY: You broke it.

    NICKY: I never touched it!

    MARY: Oh, no—it was your idea—
It was all your idea in the first place.

    NICKY: Come on—fix it.

    MARY: I don't know how to!

NICKY: Well, you could try—you could at least try!

MARY: I *am* trying....

GARY: Well...

LIZ: Yup...

GARY: They got me.

NICKY: Cause you're gonna get in trouble too, you know!

LIZ: Yup.
Looks like they got you, Tex.

MARY: Not as bad as you.

GARY: Well,
So long...

LIZ: So long, Tex...

NICKY: You got it!

GARY: Yup.

LIZ: So long, Tex.

MARY: Yeah, but Gary—it won't stabilize!

GARY: So, so, so, so, so, so, so, so, so, so, so, so, so, so, so, so....

LIZ: So how bad'd they get you?

GARY: Bad.

LIZ: Real bad?

GARY: Real, real, real bad.

MARY: Oh, nooooooo.....

NICKY: Come on, Wally—you fix it!

GARY: It was a gut shot, Tex.

MARY: I'm trying!

LIZ: Ooooooh, not the gut shot, Tex!
That's bad.

GARY: Real bad.

LIZ: Real real real bad.

GARY: Real real real real real real real real...

MARY: Oh, noooooooooooo!

(MARY *bangs the control device.*)

        MARY: Garyyyyyyyyy!

        NICKY: Whaaaaat?

LIZ: Tex, who done it to you, Tex?

        MARY: They're out of control, Gary!
        Run! Run for your life!

(NICKY *and* MARY *run off downstage right as* ZIVIA *as "Uncle Fritz" comes around the house, chasing them.*)

GARY: It was the bad guys, Tex, and they went *(Points)* thataway.

LIZ: *(Points)* Thisaway?

GARY: *(Points)* Thataway.

LIZ: *(Points)* Thisaway?

GARY: *(Points)* Thataway.

LIZ: *(Points)* Thataway?

        ZIVIA: Hoo-boy doze kitts iss dryfink me
            kraaaaaayyyyyyzy!
        Yost vait'll I get my mitts on 'em—
        Dell be a spenking dell neffa forget!

GARY: *(Points)* Thisaway.

LIZ: Whichaway?

GARY: What?

(ZIVIA *exits down right as* NICKY *as cowboy enters upstage center around house, crossing to fence.*)

NICKY: Tex! Tex! Tex! Tex! Tex!
What happened, Tex?

LIZ: They got him, Tex.

NICKY: Aw, Tex!

LIZ: They got him bad.

GARY: It was a gut shot, Tex—they got my gut!

NICKY: Who done it, Tex?

LIZ: It was the bad guys, Tex,
And they went *(Points)* thataway.

GARY: *(Points)* Thisaway.

NICKY: Whichaway?

GARY: *(Points)* Thataway.

LIZ: Whichaway?

NICKY: *(Points)* Thisaway?

GARY: *(Points)* Thataway!

LIZ: Well, don't you worry none, Tex—I aim ta git my sixgun, saddle up and ride and ride and ride and ride and ride and ride and git them bad guys got yer gut.

NICKY: You betcha, Tex—I aim ta git my sixgun too, 'n' saddle up and ride and ride and ride and ride and ride and ride some more and bang-bang-bang it 'n' shoot it and shoot-shoot-shoot some more and holler ya-hoo! Here I come ta git you bad guys got mah pardner's gut.

GARY: Aw, boys, don't leave me boys...

NICKY: Stay with him, Tex—cause he's—

GARY: Boys, cause I'm fixin to die....

LIZ: You stay with him, Tex!

NICKY: How come?

LIZ: Cause I said so.

NICKY: I'd like to see you make me.

LIZ: Them's fightin' words!

NICKY: Reach!

LIZ: Draw!

GARY: Boys, don't be fighting, boys,
Would you do that fer old Tex?
Cause he's fixin to die, boys....

NICKY: You hear...?

LIZ: Well, he look it.

GARY: Jest do me a favor, boys.

LIZ: Wah shore, Tex, shore.

GARY: Jest bury me, boys—
Would you do that for old Tex?

NICKY: Wah shore, Tex.

GARY: And tell 'em he died with his boots on—
And would you do me one more favor, boys?

LIZ: Oh, shore, Tex, shore.

GARY: Don't bury me beneath the weepin' willow tree.
Now....

You could bury me on Boot Hill er on the lone pray-ree er heck, I dunno, underneath the stars er by the shores of Gitcheegoomee er by the shining big sea water er...

NICKY: Reckon we'll jes say you died with yer boots on, Tex.

LIZ: I will.

NICKY: Heck, I will, too.

GARY: Well heck, and I'll shore be much obliged to you boys.
And I always did want to die with my boots on, too.

(MARY *enters up center around house and runs through doctor's office, chased by* ZIVIA *as "Uncle Fritz."*)

        MARY: Gary, where are you?

        ZIVIA: You krezzzy kitts kom bak!

        MARY: Gary—don't leave meeee...

        NICKY: Run, Wally!

GARY: Come to think of it, boys—would you do me just one more favor?

NICKY: Oh, shore shore shore Tex, shore.

LIZ: Whaddya want?

GARY: Well, would you not play the danged fife lowly, boys—
Now...
You kin bang the drum slowly, fellas, I won't keer...

(LIZ *is "shot."*)

LIZ: Tex?

GARY: ...heck, you kin bang it as slow as yer everlovin' western hearts desire—

LIZ: They got me, Tex.

GARY: Old Tex won't keer....

LIZ: Looks like they got me worse than Tex.

NICKY: Worse than Tex?

GARY: Worse than who?

LIZ: You callin' me a liar?

GARY: You callin' me a liar?

NICKY: Who's callin' who a liar?

LIZ: I dunno, but they's fightin' words.

GARY: Reach!

LIZ: Draw!

NICKY: Awwwwwwwwwwwwwwww...

(NICKY *is "shot."*)

NICKY: Ya got me, Tex and Tex.

LIZ: We didn't mean to, Tex.

GARY: You was in the crossfire, Tex!

NICKY: You got me worse than both of ya put together!

GARY: Aw, that's a load a bull.

NICKY: Turn my face to the wall, Tex!

LIZ: You ain't hurt so bad.

NICKY: Hey Tex!

(ZIVIA *as "Uncle Fritz" enters the doctor's office.*)

> ZIVIA: Hoo-boy doze kitts iss dryfink me kraaaaaayyyyyyzy!

NICKY: Hey, turn my face to the wall!

LIZ: Y'ain't hurt so bad as us, ya sissy.

NICKY: Whoooooooooooo—that smarts!

> ZIVIA: Yost vait'll I get my mitts on 'em—
> Dell be a spenking dell neffa forget!

GARY: T'ain't nothing but a flesh wound, anyway!

> ZIVIA: *Ach du lieber* dees krezzy kits yost lookit det mess day made mine *gott in himmel*—
> *Und meine* machine *kaput!*
> *Jahvohl! Dass ist ein* fol-desaster.
> *Aber*—hmmm...*ja* vell dis is mebbe not zo bet. Hmf...!
> I am tinking...mebby eef I tinker little bit mit dees ting, und...(*ja, ja, ja*) over here little bit and *ja* (*das* is not zo *gut* but...) oh vell...
> Now den,
> Vere is dat deGaussing unit?

(ZIVIA *fixes control device.*)

LIZ: Reckon yer daid, Tex.

GARY: Yup.

NICKY: Yup.

LIZ: Yup.

NICKY: Yup.

GARY: Yup.
Reckon I am, Tex.

NICKY: Yup.
I reckon I am, Tex, too.

GARY: Ya like it much?

NICKY: Nope.

LIZ: Nope.

NICKY: I feel so lonesome I could cry, Tex.

LIZ: Yup.

NICKY: I feel so lonesome I could cry.

GARY: Git along little dogie.

NICKY: Down in the valley
Down in the valley
Down in the valley

LIZ: Yippie-yi-yo-kye-yay, Tex.

NICKY: I feel so lonesome I could cry.

LIZ: Yup.

GARY: Yup.

LIZ: Yup.

GARY: Yup.

LIZ: Yup.

NICKY: Down in the valley
Down in the valley

GARY: Git along little dogie.

LIZ: Yippie-yi-yo-kye-yay, Tex...

GARY: Well, so long, Tex.

NICKY: Well...

LIZ: Yup...

NICKY: So long...
Well,

LIZ: So long, Tex.

GARY: Well...

NICKY: Yup...

LIZ: So long...

GARY: Well, so long, Tex.

NICKY: So long.

LIZ: So long, Tex...

ZIVIA: *Ja*, zo, dass pretty *gut*, now.

*(Fade out)*

END OF PLAY

# CRAZY PLAY #36

# DIABOLICAL TALES FROM BAYONNE

## ACT ONE

*(In the house:* MARY *and* LIZ *in the rear window,* GARY *on sofa)*

        LIZ: But?...

        MARY: But?...

        LIZ: Is this it?

        MARY: Is this—

        LIZ: The end?

GARY: Help me!

        MARY: Oh, God.

        LIZ: Oh, God.

        MARY: Oh, God, this is it, this is the end, it really is.

NICKY: *(Off)* Hang on, Dad!

        LIZ: It really is.

GARY: Somebody!

        LIZ: I'm a goner.

NICKY: *(Off)* Coming!

        LIZ: I'm a goner now...

GARY: Oh, hurry—God help me!
Please help me!
Please hurry!

        MARY: I'm going to lie down now...

        LIZ: Just lie down peacefully...

        MARY: In agony and pain...

        LIZ: And wait...

GARY: Help me!

    LIZ: Wait for the end.

NICKY: *(Off)* Hang on, Dad!

    MARY: The end is very very near...

    LIZ: The end is nigh...

GARY: Somebody!

NICKY: *(Off)* Coming!

    LIZ: Oh God—I'm dying

    MARY: I'm in agony

    LIZ: This is suffering

    MARY: I'm suffering...

    LIZ: My god, how I'm suffering!

GARY: Oh, hurry—God help me!
Please help me!
Please hurry!
Help me!

    MARY: The light is growing dim...

NICKY: *(Off)* Hang on, Dad!

    MARY: My pulse is getting weak...

GARY: Somebody!

NICKY: *(Off)* Coming!

GARY: Oh, hurry—God help me!
Please help me!
Please hurry!

    LIZ: Oh, God, what tragedy—but no, don't weep—don't weep for me...

GARY: Help me!

    MARY: This is the end, Lord—

    LIZ: Koom-bye-yah...

NICKY: *(Off)* Hang on, Dad!

    MARY: I hear those voices calling for me, Lord.

GARY: Somebody!

    LIZ: Take me, Jesus!

NICKY: *(Off)* Coming!

      MARY: Take me Lord...

GARY: Oh, hurry—God help me!

      LIZ: I'm goin' home...

GARY: Please help me!
Please hurry!

      LIZ: But?...

      MARY: But?...

      LIZ: Is this it?

      MARY: Is this—

*(GARY falls off the sofa and onto the floor.)*

      LIZ: The end?

GARY: Help me!

*(Blackout)*

## ACT TWO

*(In the house: GARY on sofa, NICKY by the door)*

NICKY: Gee but it's great to be back home, Dad,
Even though I guess I've been a disappointment to you.

GARY: You've been a giant disappointment to me, son.

*(MARY and LIZ look in upstage window.)*

      LIZ: But...

      MARY: But....

GARY: Did you hear that?

NICKY: Hunh?

      LIZ: Is this it?

GARY: I said you've been a giant disappointment to me.

NICKY: Hunh?

      MARY: Is this—

GARY: A disappointment—
You're just a giant fucking disappointment to me, son, is what I'm saying—

NICKY: Hunh?

LIZ: The end?

GARY: You bring me down, ok?—whenever I see you, son,
You just bring me down so bad, you really do.

NICKY: Hunh?

GARY: And you're so stupid.

NICKY: Hunh?

GARY: I said you're stupid—you're really stupid—
You're the stupidest person I ever met in my life!

NICKY: Hunh?

GARY: Just forget it, son—forget it.

NICKY: Gee, but it's great to be back home, Dad,
Even though I guess I've been a disappointment to you.

GARY: You been a *major* disappointment is what I'm saying.

NICKY: Hunh?

GARY: Forget it, will you?
*(He crosses to downstage center window.)*

NICKY: Gee, but it's great to be back home.

LIZ: But...

NICKY: Hey, Dad?

MARY: But?...

NICKY: Dad?

LIZ: Is this it?

GARY: (Sheesh—this upset stomach's really getting to me...)

NICKY: Dad?

GARY: Shut up!
(I feel...terrible, this gas pain is—Whoa!—)
(Really making me nauseous—)

MARY: Is this—

NICKY: Hey, Dad?

GARY: Shut up!

LIZ: The end?

NICKY: Hey, tell me a story, Dad.

GARY: Drop dead!

NICKY: Hey, Dad?

GARY: (Sure wish I could just lie down....)

NICKY: Hey, tell me the story of how I was born...

*(Blackout)*

## ACT THREE

*(In the doctor's office:* ZIVIA *at the desk)*

ZIVIA: Come in.
Come in...
Come in, please.
Hello?
*(Rising)* Come in?
Come in, please...
Hello?
Come in....?

*(*ZIVIA *exits down right as* MARY *and* LIZ *as* BOB *and* BILL *enter up center, dancing.)*

LIZ: Well, howdy, Bob.

MARY: Hello there, Bill.

LIZ: So how's your brand new face?

MARY: It's broken, Bill.

LIZ: I thought so, Bob.

MARY: So whattaya think about that?

LIZ: Hey, d'ja hear the news?

MARY: No, what's the news?

LIZ: Well, your house burned down last night.

MARY: Gee, I feel real bad.

LIZ: Yeah, you look real bad.

MARY: Hey, and I got a train to catch.

LIZ: You're a hard man, Bob.

MARY: I'm a card man, Bill.

LIZ: You're a carp man, Bob.

MARY: I'm a harp man, Bill.

LIZ: You're a hash man, Bob.

MARY: I'm a wash man, Bill.

LIZ: You're a wish man, Bob.

MARY: I'm a wise man, Bill.
Call me hard, harp, hasp, wasp, wisp, wise.

LIZ: I'll call you hard, herd, held, weld, wile, wise.

MARY: Just call me hard, card, care, cape, wipe, wise.

LIZ: I'll call you hard, hare, hire, hide, wide, wise.

MARY: Say, Bill?

LIZ: Yeah, Bob?...

MARY: Forget it.
Say, Bill?

LIZ: Yeah, Bob?...

MARY: Forget it.

LIZ: Say, Bob?

MARY: Yeah, Bill...

LIZ: Forget it.
Say, Bob?

MARY: Yeah, Bill?...

LIZ: Say, Bob?

MARY: Yeah, Bill?

*(In the doctor's office: ZIVIA has entered down right followed by GARY; MARY and LIZ watch the next scene.)*

GARY: See, it's about my...

ZIVIA: What?

GARY: ...you know....

ZIVIA: Your you-know?
And a mighty fine you-know it is at that, I'll betcha.
So—why don't you show it to me, Big Guy? Hmmmmm?

GARY: Jeez—you're blowing my mind, Doc.

ZIVIA: Hey, who's gonna know?

GARY: You blow me away, you crazy Doctor.

ZIVIA: Show me, Big Guy!

GARY: Stop already!

ZIVIA: Wanna see your disease!

GARY: Stop, stop, you crazy doctor!

ZIVIA: Show me, Big Guy—show me now...!

(ZIVIA *chases* GARY *off up center;* MARY *and* LIZ *resume dancing.*)

LIZ: Sure is an odd world, Bob.

MARY: Sure is an old world, Bill.

LIZ: Sure is a cold world, Bob.

MARY: Sure is a cola world, Bill.

LIZ: Singin diddy-wah,

MARY: Diddy-wah diddy.

LIZ: Singin diddy-wah,

MARY: Diddy-wah diddy.

LIZ: Singin diddy-wah,

MARY: Diddy-wah diddy.

LIZ: Singin diddy-wah-diddy all day.

*(Blackout)*

## ACT FOUR

(GARY *and* ZIVIA *in the doctor's office*)

ZIVIA: So, uh, tell me—
What exactly would you say your problem was?

GARY: Well, I uh—sheesh, I really hate to uh, hate to uh...

ZIVIA: Speculate on that?

GARY: Yeah, well I uh—
You don't mind if I call you doc do you doc?

ZIVIA: Beg your pardon?

GARY: Call you doc?

ZIVIA: Well, yes, I am the doctor, but uh....
Well, I think we're uh... getting a little off-course here.

GARY: Un-hunh...

ZIVIA: So, uh...

Where were we...?

GARY: Well I, uh...we were talking about my problem...

ZIVIA: Yeah, your problem—
What's your problem, I forget?

GARY: Well, let me put it to you honest, Doc.
Let me put it to you straightforward and man to man, if I may.

ZIVIA: I wish you would.

GARY: Last night I had a dream.
Thought a little dog was chewing my dick.
Thought a little um, uh...

ZIVIA: A little dog, did you say?

GARY: Yeah, a little...uh,
Whattya call em?

ZIVIA: Pekinese?

GARY: No, like a...

ZIVIA: Chihuahua? Dachshund?

GARY: No, like a Weimareiner, I think.

ZIVIA: But a Weimareiner, that's like a huge....

GARY: Oh, yeah?
So what's a Pekinese? Is that like....?

(LIZ and MARY as BOB and BILL enter up center, dancing.)

> LIZ: Hey—d'ja hear the news?
>
> MARY: No, what's the news?
>
> LIZ: There's a brand new gal in town.
>
> MARY: Is her name Marie?
>
> LIZ: No, her name's Maroon.
>
> MARY: Aw, then I don't want to know her.
>
> LIZ: How's your dear old wife?

MARY: Well, she ain't so hot.

LIZ: Yeah, that's what I thought, too.

MARY: How's yer old bag?

LIZ: She's lot like yours.

MARY: Well, I heard she was hibbity.

LIZ: That's an odd word, Bob.

MARY: It's an old word, Bill.

LIZ: That's a gold word, Bob.

MARY: It's a good word, Bill.
Call me hard, hand, wand, wind, wine, wise.

LIZ: I'll call you hard, bard, bare, base, vase, vise, wise.

MARY: Just call me hard, lard, lord, word, wore, wire, wise.

LIZ: I'll call you hard, pard, pare, rare, race, rice, rise, wise.

MARY: Say, Bill?

LIZ: Yeah, Bob...

MARY: Forget it.

LIZ: Say, Bob?

MARY: Yeah, Bill...

LIZ: Forget it.

MARY: Say, Bill?

LIZ: Yeah, Bob...

MARY: Forget it.

LIZ: Say, Bob?

MARY: Yeah, Bill...

LIZ: Forget it.

GARY: But isn't it going to hurt?

ZIVIA: Trust me.

GARY: Really?

ZIVIA: Well, you may feel it, but...

GARY: But it isn't going to hurt?

ZIVIA: No, not much.

GARY: What do you mean, not much?—

ZIVIA: Maybe a little prick.

GARY: Doc—level with me, Doc:
How much is it really going to hurt?

ZIVIA: As I said—you'll feel it—you'll feel discomfort...
Some momentary discomfort...

GARY: It's really going to hurt, isn't it?

ZIVIA: Look—we'll give you something for the pain.

GARY: It's that bad?

ZIVIA: Sir, I have to make a diagnosis—
Now this is a standard procedure, we use a local anesthetic....

GARY: I want a general.

ZIVIA: I'm sorry, that's not possible.

GARY: I want a general.

ZIVIA: Sir, that is simply not possible with this procedure, I'm sorry.

GARY: Why not?

ZIVIA: Because we need to know what you're feeling.

GARY: So there is pain.

ZIVIA: Sir—believe me—the pain isn't going to be the problem!
Excuse me while I make a quick call—
*(She picks up the telephone.)*

GARY: Then what is gonna be the problem, Doctor?

ZIVIA: (Hi, it's me.)
(You busy?)

GARY: Doc????

*(LIZ and MARY exit dancing.)*

        LIZ: Singin diddy-wah,

        MARY: Diddy-wah diddy.

        LIZ: Singin diddy-wah,

        MARY: Diddy-wah diddy.

LIZ: Singin diddy-wah,

MARY: Diddy-wah diddy.

LIZ: Singin diddy-wah-diddy all day.

(ZIVIA *is no longer on the phone.*)

GARY: Months?

ZIVIA: Oh, gee, I....

GARY: Weeks?

ZIVIA: Well, maybe...yeah, maybe weeks...

GARY: But no treatment at all, none at all—I mean I just can't believe that, Doctor.

ZIVIA: But see when you say "treatment"—
I mean, technically speaking, there are procedures but..

GARY: What?

ZIVIA: Well, I'm afraid they'd only be a waste of time.

GARY: Could I maybe get a second opinion?

ZIVIA: Fine.
*(She picks up the telephone.)*

GARY: I mean, you know, just to be sure.

ZIVIA: I'm sorry, I really do have to make a call....

GARY: You are mad at me, aren't you?

ZIVIA: (Hi, it's me.)

GARY: See I'm just so... *(Mumbles)*

ZIVIA: Beg your pardon?
(Yeah, I'm with a patient)

GARY: Scared, I'm just so scared, I'm just so scared!

ZIVIA: Well, of course you are and you have every right to be.

*(Fade out)*


## ACT FIVE

(LIZ *and* MARY *as* BOB *and* BILL)

MARY: Okay—just ask me anything, Bill—
Just ask me anything at all.

LIZ: Okay, Bob.

> MARY: Ask me anything your little heart desires...
>
> LIZ: All right, I will.
>
> Say, Bob—am I on time?
>
> MARY: Oh, yes, yes, yes, you naughty boy—you know you are.
>
> LIZ: Well then, have I been going in the wrong direction, Bob?
>
> MARY: Oh, yes, yes, yes, you naughty boy—you know you have.
>
> LIZ: But whattya think, Bob—does this tie go with my suspenders?
>
> MARY: Oh, yes, yes, yes, you naughty boy—you know it does.
>
> LIZ: Gee Bob, should I be cheating maybe on my income taxes?
>
> MARY: Oh, yes, yes, yes, you naughty boy—you know you should.

*(In the doctor's office: ZIVIA on phone)*

ZIVIA: (...I'm sure you do, hon...)
(...I'm sure you do.)

> LIZ: Uhhhhhh, will the swallows be coming back to Capistrano in the year 2929, Bob?

ZIVIA: (...Yes I do, Randy.)

> MARY: Oh, yes, yes, yes, you naughty boy—you know they will.

ZIVIA: (...If you'll let me...)

> LIZ: Say—does anybody here know Mary, Mary Wang?

ZIVIA: (Would you let me explain?)

> MARY: Oh, yes, yes, yes, you naughty boy—you know they do.

ZIVIA: (I mean, what do you think we've been doing for two years?)

> LIZ: My god, my god—is this a dagger that I see before me?

*(In the doctor's office, GARY approaches desk and sits; MARY and LIZ watch the scene.)*

ZIVIA: Hi, I'm Doctor Scott.

GARY: Doctor...

ZIVIA: Monica, just call me Monica.

> LIZ: But where will it lead, Bob?
> And what does it all add up to, Bob?
> And Bob—
> How did everything get this way?

ZIVIA: I'll be with you in a moment.

GARY: Okay, Doc.

> MARY: Hey—good questions, Bill!

> LIZ: But what are my responsibilities, Bob?
> And what should I do about them, Bob?
> And Bob—is there reason for hope?

ZIVIA: (Did you read the book, honey—did you read the book I gave you?)

> MARY: Good questions, Bill...
> Good questions, Bill...
> Good questions, Bill...

ZIVIA: (Randy—I'm with a patient—
Read the book.)
*(She hangs up.)*
So—what's troubling us, hunh?
What's on our mind, today?

GARY: Well, Doc, it's this way...

ZIVIA: Something medical, I'm guessing? Something that might need a little, uh—
Medical attention...?
Okay—make yourself comfortable.

GARY: ...Kinda hard to talk about.

ZIVIA: Un-hunh...

GARY: I'm just so scared there's something really wrong with me.

ZIVIA: I tell you what—
Why don't we let me be the judge of that, okay? After all, I am the doctor.
So, would you like me to examine you, hunh?
You like a little examination?

GARY: I dunno...

ZIVIA: Sure you would.
Everybody goes for a little examination.

GARY: Okay.

ZIVIA: You know I should probably explain—if I seem a little distracted you know—
It's 'cause I'm getting married in three weeks.

GARY: Oh, that's great, congratulations.

ZIVIA: Oh, thank you, thank you, I know—he's a really great guy—I mean we've known each other for years, you know—
And we dated and stuff, you know...
*(She exits down right as she talks.)*
But, with like you know *my* schedule and *his* schedule it was really hard.
So about a year ago we broke up and I don't know he went out with other people and I went out with other people but you know we kept bumping into each other, so one day he asked me to go on a fishing cruise with him to the Gulf of Mexico, you know—

GARY: Doc?

ZIVIA: *(Off)* Deep sea fishing, you know...?
And I thought oh my god the last thing in the world I want to do is be stuck on a fishing boat with Randy (that's his name)....

GARY: I got that thing, Doc.

ZIVIA: *(Off)* Un-hunh.
But he said we'd have separate cabins so I thought—oh, okay, why not— and you know I was amazed, it was really fabulous.

GARY: Doc I got that thing!

*(ZIVIA enters left with a very large syringe.)*

ZIVIA: You ever been deep sea fishing?

GARY: Help me, Doc—I got that thing!

ZIVIA: What thing?

GARY: That thing, you know—that thing!
I got that thing!

ZIVIA: Oh, god...
You poor, poor man...

GARY: Please help me, Doc, I'm scared, I'm really scared.

ZIVIA: You poor poor thing...

GARY: Don't wanna die, Doc—please don't let me die!

ZIVIA: You poor poor man, you poor poor thing.

*(In the landscape:* LIZ *and* MARY *resume dancing.)*

LIZ: So, howdy, Bob.

MARY: Say, howdy, Bill.

LIZ: Here's the hundred bucks I owe you.

MARY: How's your mother, Bill?

LIZ: She's dying, Bob.

MARY: Here's your hundred dollars back.

LIZ: Hey, I like the hat.

MARY: Hey, it's yours, my friend.

LIZ: Gee, thanks—so how do I look?

MARY: Hey, I like the hat.

LIZ: Hey, it's yours, my friend.

MARY: Naw—you ain't gonna catch me twice!!!

LIZ: Cause it's odd work, Bob.

MARY: And it's old work, Bill.

LIZ: And it's bold work, Bob.

MARY: And it's bolo work, Bill.

LIZ: Say, Bob?

MARY: Yeah, Bill?...

LIZ: Forget it.
Say, Bob?

MARY: Yeah, Bill?...

LIZ: Forget it.

MARY: Say, Bill?

LIZ: Yeah, Bob...

MARY: Forget it.
Say, Bill?

LIZ: Yeah, Bob?...

MARY: Say, Bill?

LIZ: Yeah, Bob?

MARY: You're a hard man, Bill.

LIZ: No, I'm a yard man, Bob.

MARY: But you're a yarn man, Bill.

LIZ: No, I'm a barn man, Bob.

MARY: But you're a bare man, Bill.

LIZ: No, I'm a base man, Bob.

MARY: Well, you're a bise man, Bill.

LIZ: No, I'm a wise man, Bob.
Just call me hard, fard, fire, fife, wife, wise.

MARY: I'll call you hard, hart, wart, ware, wave, wive, wise.

LIZ: Just call me hard, hara, rara, rare, rape, ripe, and wipe wise

MARY: I'll call you hard, hark, mark, mask, musk, muse, and mise wise

*(Office: ZIVIA on the phone)*

ZIVIA: (Honey, I really need to have that shower, it's like a big deal thing for me.)

GARY: Doc, could I just...uh, maybe before I go and all, could I show ya my...?

LIZ: ...Diddy-wah

ZIVIA: Beg your pardon?

LIZ: ...Diddy-wah

GARY: Show you my...

ZIVIA: What?

LIZ: ...Diddy-wah

ZIVIA: What? What?

LIZ: ...Diddy-wah

GARY: Well, my...you-know.

LIZ: ...Diddy-wah,

MARY: Diddy-wah diddy.

LIZ: Singin diddy-wah,

MARY: Diddy-wah diddy.

LIZ: Singin diddy-wah,

MARY: Diddy-wah diddy.

LIZ: Singin diddy-wah-diddy all day.

*(Blackout)*

## ACT SIX

*(Voices in the blackout)*

MARY: Well, could you squeeze me in at *ten*?

LIZ: Darling, I'm having a *hair* wax at ten...

MARY: So, then—squeeze me in at *eleven*, dah-ling.

LIZ: But darling, I have to see Carlo's new *line* at eleven
Something fresh and godawful in *cruise*wear, I'm told,
So I'll need a little lie-down for at *least* an hour after.
But I could squeeze you in...say, *two*-ish?

MARY: But darling, at *twoish* I'm golfing with Pepe till *four*.
Then at *four* I'm with Nina for skeet until *five*.
Then at *five* I'm with Jurgen and someone named *Soto* who's here for a run
   at the *Kaiserring*—or is that next week?
Oh, that's next week—never mind.
Darling—why don't you squeeze me in at five?

LIZ: Five....
Five five five five five—
Oh foo—darling this is wretched, this was not meant to *be*.
Poor wretched *Fifi* made me promise to help her find a new girl *weeks* ago
   and I *can't* let her down after what she's *been* through,
But listen—I'll meet you anywhere on god's *earth*, darling, after six.

MARY: Six is the potlach—how could you forget?

LIZ: Of course, how silly of me.

MARY: Because you couldn't go—remember—you had *gardening* class or
   *mambo* class or *cigarette-rolling* class, or....

LIZ: *Weatherstripping*, darling.

MARY: Mmm...

LIZ: What about Sunday?

MARY: I don't think so.

LIZ: I could squeeze you in.

MARY: I don't think so.

LIZ: Are you absolutely absolutely about Sunday?

MARY: Monica, I do not think so.

LIZ: You're *sure*, darling?

MARY: *Positive*, darling.

LIZ: Might one inquire?
Well?
Darling, don't be a *pill*...

*(Lights up: in the house, ZIVIA, MARY and LIZ on the sofa)*

ZIVIA: Well, I had a bad experience lately....

LIZ: Tell, tell!

ZIVIA: I had a guy just come apart all over me.
It was so weird—
He wasn't leaking or anything, he just—
All of a sudden, he just like came apart at the seams.

And I had a good firm grip on him, too.

LIZ: My God, it sounds awful, poor Monica.

ZIVIA: Ruined my slacks.

MARY: It doesn't surprise me, not any more.

ZIVIA: But I never knew things like that happened.
And apparently they happen all the time.

MARY: Darling I would believe anything these days, I swear.

LIZ: French guy, hon?
Was he French?

ZIVIA: Well, it's not as if we were properly introduced.

LIZ: French guys—happens all the time.
God, I hope you were protected, Monica.

MARY: You were protected, weren't you, Monica?

ZIVIA: Well, I'm *covered*, Monica, if that's what you mean.

LIZ: Monica, don't be a loser.

MARY: Yeah, nobody loves a loser, Monica.

LIZ: We're actually rather concerned about you, Monica.
Do I have bags?

MARY: You look fine. Why?

LIZ: I feel puffy, like I've got bags—
I wonder why?

MARY: Why what?

LIZ: Why I've got bags.

MARY: But, darling, you don't have bags.

LIZ: I know, that's what you *told* me, darling.

MARY: So who said you had bags?

LIZ: Nobody.

MARY: Oh.

(ZIVIA *gets up and crosses to the bay window.*)

ZIVIA: I'm sorry, you guys—I gotta get out of here.
I mean, I gotta do something with my life, okay?
I mean, like something meaningful.
You know?
Like sometimes I think about—
Well,
Like about the third world for example.
I mean, the oppression, all the suffering going on and stuff—

(*In the landscape,* GARY *crosses toward house.*)

      GARY: Doc, I don't feel right.

ZIVIA: I mean—those are people just like us.

MARY: No, they're not, Monica.

      GARY: I don't feel too good, Doc.

ZIVIA: Okay, I mean maybe the situation is a little different
With the economic and the political but—

MARY: They are *not like us.*

      GARY: Something's going on inside of
       me, Doc, I don't feel right.

ZIVIA: Okay, but don't you ever *think* about stuff like that?

LIZ: I do.

      GARY: Something's changing in there,
       Doc—d'yunnerstan?

LIZ: Monica doesn't, I don't think but...

MARY: No, but I *work* with people every *day.*

ZIVIA: Well, so do I, okay?

GARY: What's wrong with me, Doc?

LIZ: Oh, Monica, can't you just forget about it?

(GARY *kneels in front of bay window, curling into a ball.*)

> GARY: Oh please tell me, please tell me what's wrong.
> Please—I don't wanna die, Doc.
> There's something in there, isn't there—
> Oh, Doc, it's gonna kill me, and I'm scared, I'm scared, I'm really scared, I don't wanna die—
> Please help me, Doc, I don't want to die...
> There's gotta be something...

ZIVIA: Why, you poor poor man.

> GARY: Don't let me die, Doc—please don't let me die.

ZIVIA: Why, you poor poor thing.

> GARY: There's gotta be something you can do....
> Ya gotta help me, Doc, please help me, please don't let me die.

> ZIVIA: You poor poor man, you poor poor thing.
> You poor poor man.

(NICKY *enters upstage, crossing down as he talks to audience.*)

NICKY: Ladies and gentlemen—
I know something....
Something about each and every one of you—
Something you may not even know about yourselves—
And it's good news, it's such exciting news....
Because what I know can change your life right now and start you climbing up the stairway to success:
But first let me explain—
This not a get-rich-quick scheme or a way to live longer, or to achieve glamor or power or fame in life—
Although many of you will indeed achieve these things
Simply by taking advantage of the knowledge I'm about to share with you tonight.

(*In the house:* LIZ *and* MARY *join* ZIVIA *at the bay window.*)

> GARY: Bury me, Tex...

NICKY: Now, isn't that good news?

> GARY: Please bury me, Tex...

NICKY: Yes, isn't that exciting news?

LIZ: So long, pardner...

MARY: So long, cowboy.

NICKY: And suppose tonight that I could show you how to obtain any success, any achievement or goal in life that you could ever have in mind?
Would it be worth your while to listen?

LIZ: So long, pardner..

NICKY: Oh, friends—I have a good good feeling,
Such a good good feeling about each and every one of you tonight and you know why?
Because of the Success Knowledge that is already in this room, already working inside each and every one of you right now.
But how will you use it?
How will you use this precious knowledge?

MARY: So long, cowboy.

NICKY: Only time will tell and only you can decide.
How many people here want more from life?
No, no—don't answer me.
I want you to think about this—really think about this:
Do you believe that it's possible
To change your life?
Are you *prepared*
To change your life?
Can you honestly say—
I want to change my life?
Now, just think about that for a moment—think about it—
And I'll be right back to tell you more.

*(Fadeout)*

END OF PLAY

# CRAZY PLAY #45

## MOM'S SUBMARINE WORLD AND HOUSE OF STRANGENESS

### ACT ONE

*(In the landscape, ZIVIA and GARY as cowboys; in the house, MARY and LIZ on sofa.)*

                      ZIVIA: Sure is hot.

                      GARY: What?

                      ZIVIA: Said it's hot.

MARY: Hey, Dad?

                      GARY: Yup...

MARY: Hey, tell me a story, Dad.

LIZ: My boy, let me tell you a story—

                      GARY: That's what I thought you said.

LIZ: Let me tell you the story of how you were born!

MARY: (Oh, Jeez—not that again!)

                      ZIVIA: I said it and I mean it, mister.

LIZ: My boy—did I ever tell you the story of how you were born?

MARY: (Only about a hundred million times!)

LIZ: No, I don't suppose I ever did—heh heh heh—
Guess it must have slipped my mind—heh heh heh—wonder why?

MARY: Hunh?

                      ZIVIA: And now I'm gonna kill ya.

                      GARY: Hunh?

LIZ: I said I wonder why it slipped my mind I wonder why?

MARY: (Who cares?)
*(She gets up and crosses to bay window.)*

       ZIVIA: I said I'm gonna kill ya, Mister.

LIZ: Well, anyway, one day when I was down at the plant,
When I was down at the rotating plant one day just rolling round in a bucket of slime called somebody special,
I was suddenly overcome by an urge to fornicate with a steam table!
Haw-haw—did I say railroad car?—haw-haw—
I guess I really meant the boot inspector—haw-haw-haw—

MARY: (Why does he do this to me?)

LIZ: Guess I really meant the shore patrol! Oh, lordy me—
Guess what I really meant was something the cat dragged in!
Har, har, har, har...(chuffa chuffa chuffa)...

MARY: (Why does he talk to me this way and shoot me those strange glances?)

LIZ: Son, I must confess to you that sometimes words come out of my mouth which I did not put there and this is the source of considerable embarrassment to me...

MARY: (Why do I find it so hard to pay attention to this man?)

LIZ: Son—pay attention to me, son—

       GARY: You must be the new kid I been
        hearin' about.

LIZ: Pay attention to your aged father...

       ZIVIA: Yeah I'm the new kid, all right,
        I'm the new kid.

MARY: (Why do I have the feeling that I know this man?)

       GARY: Heard tell you was handy, too—
        handy with a six gun—
       Singing ti-yi-yippie-yippie-yippie-
        yippie-yay.

MARY: (Yeah—wait a minute—maybe he's right—)

       ZIVIA: Well maybe I am and maybe I ain't,
       But I'm the new kid, mister.

MARY: (Maybe it's been my fault all along!)

       ZIVIA: Ain't I the new kid, mister?

MARY: (Maybe if I'd really loved him, this would never have happened....)

LIZ: My boy did I ever tell you about the time you were born?
I was wrapping a present for somebody special,
When I suddenly become obsessed with the idea of bending a wire
    coat-hanger against my face and calling it a personal statement....
Son, I'm a boring old fart and my kidneys are shot
But I beg you, I plead you, I need you to loan me some money.

                        GARY: You gonna shoot me now, sonny?

LIZ: Would you spot your dear old Dad a couple of bucks for a bottle-a
    cheap wine?...

MARY: (Naaaaaah!)

                        GARY: Gonna shoot-shoot, sonny—gonna
                            click-it?

(MARY *leaves house*)

LIZ: Wait—son—did I ever did I ever tell you bout the time you were born?
I was standing in hip-waders—some kind of rubberized—
Standing in shit—I was up to my ass in it!
All of a sudden the craving comes over me
Gut-churning yearning for speed started burning me
(*Sheesh—this upset stomach's really...*)

                        ZIVIA: Get ready to die, pop.

LIZ: Hadda be moving at ninety miles an hour, son, I had that need so bad,
    it was so bad...

                        GARY: Don't shoot me, Mister.

                        ZIVIA: Ya ready to die?

LIZ: (God, I feel...terrible—Whoa!—really nauseous...)

                        GARY: Please don't shoot me don't shoot me
                            don't shoot me down like a dog, Mister.

                        ZIVIA: Ya ready to die?

LIZ: Ever tried a slice of that pink meat, sonny?
Whoa-whooooa-whoooooaaa-whoooooooaaaaaaa, boy—

(LIZ *collapses on the floor as* GARY *dies in slow motion.*)

LIZ: (Hoo boy—I don't *know*—what the hell did I eat...?)

                        ZIVIA: Ya know what they call the wind,
                            pop?

LIZ: Lemme ask ya, son—ever taste some of that—
(Christ—I'm all clammy!)

                        ZIVIA: They call the wind Maree-ya.

*(Fadeout)*

## ACT TWO

*(In the doctor's office:* MARY *and* NICKY *as sailors; in the landscape,* ZIVIA *and* LIZ *as cowboys )*

MARY: Captain?

NICKY: Speak up, there, sailor.
I can tell there's something hot and nasty boiling up inside you that you've got to get off your chest.

MARY: Well, sir, it's...not an easy thing to talk about.

NICKY: Forget these bars and give it to me straight, son.

MARY: Well, it's this way, sir.

> ZIVIA: *Alors*, Tex...
>
> LIZ: *Oui*....

MARY: I mean, me and the men, me and the men know there's an asteroid hurtling at us from the depths of space at oh, about a hundred million miles an hour, sir, and all that that implies....

> ZIVIA: *Salut.*

NICKY: Check....

> LIZ: *Salut*, Tex!
>
> ZIVIA: *Oui*...
>
> LIZ: *Alors*...

MARY: And we know we're outmanned and outgunned and hopelessly outnumbered and all that kind of stuff...

> ZIVIA: *Salut*, Tex.

NICKY: Check...

> LIZ: *Alors, salut.*
>
> ZIVIA: *Oui.*
>
> LIZ: *Bon.*

MARY: I mean, we know it's basically curtains for us, sir...

NICKY: Check...

> LIZ: *Alors, salut.*
>
> ZIVIA: *Oui.*

LIZ: *Bon.*

MARY: But Captain—what's all this scuttlebutt about Dad?

LIZ: *Ça va?*

ZIVIA: *Ça va.*

NICKY: Can you keep a secret?

MARY: Yes, sir—I think so.

NICKY: Dad's dead, sailor.

ZIVIA: *Mais alors, dis-donc...*

NICKY: Now don't go all to pieces on me, son.
That's all there is to be said about it.

MARY: Not exactly, sir.

ZIVIA: *Ça va?*

LIZ: *Ça va.*

MARY: I mean, me and the men, you see, me and the men know he's dead,
But what we heard was....

NICKY: Forget what you heard, yeoman, and that's a direct order.
Just break it off, chew it, spit it out in a paper bag or what have you, burn the bag and put it in another bag and throw the whole damned thing over the side.
That's a D O D directive, top priority, your eyes only.
From now on, brass wants dead dead, just like in the old days, just like it used to be and it's our job to get us back there.

MARY: Aye-aye, sir.

LIZ: *Eh bien...*

NICKY: Of course, off the record and on a personal note, I just hope you weren't emotionally close to or in some other way mixed-up with the deceased.

ZIVIA: *Eh bien...*

MARY: No sir, we were friends—

LIZ: *Eh bien...*

MARY: I wouldn't say good friends, sir—just friends, like maybe two, three hundred other pretty cool guys on the ship.

NICKY: Then let's keep it that way, shall we?

(ZIVIA *and* MARY *sing and dance a little hornpipe, as* NICKY *and* MARY *watch.*)

ZIVIA: *J'avais ma mule*
*Elle s'appelle "Sal"*
*Quinze kilometres au*
*L'Erie Canal*

LIZ: *Elle travaille forte*
*Et amicale*
*Quinze kilometres au*
*L'Erie Canal*

BOTH: *Pont bas! Tout le monde descend.*
*Pont bas! On est navigant.*
*Et on y connait ses voisins et on y connait ses copains*
*En faisant un petit passage au l'Erie canal...*
*La la-la-la la la-la-la*
*La la-la la la la-la-la la*
*La la-la-la la la la-la*
*La la-la la la la-la-la la (Etc...)*

NICKY: Now what the hell is their problem?

MARY: You mean, those people waving on the shore?

NICKY: Check.

MARY: Well, sir, I believe they are welcoming us.

NICKY: Sure they are, sailor—but where? Hmmmmmmmmmmmmm?

MARY: Well, sir, I believe they call this France.

>LIZ: *Oui, mais...*

>ZIVIA: *Eh bien...*

>LIZ: *Ça va?*

>ZIVIA: *Alors...*

>LIZ: *A tout a l'heure.*

NICKY: Right—where the French people live—I've heard of that...

>ZIVIA: *A tout a l'heure*, Tex.

MARY: That's the general idea, sir.

NICKY: Women wear no pants, that type of deal?

>LIZ: *Oui*, Tex—*a tout a l'heure.*

MARY: Gee, sir, I'm just an enlisted man.

NICKY: Stand easy, sailor—hey, let's toss one of those ropes or whatever you call 'em over the front of this thing...

MARY: Heave a line from the bow, sir?

NICKY: Yeah, just tie this sucker up and let's go check the place out. You got any protection, son?

MARY: Well, sir, I always carry a condom and an automatic on shore leave— just in case, you never know.

NICKY: Hey—that's nice, I like that son, I like your style.

*(Fade out)*

## ACT THREE

*(In the landscape,* LIZ, NICKY, GARY *and* MARY *as cowboys)*

LIZ: Heard tell there was a man in Dodge was fast.

NICKY: Could be.

LIZ: Could be you was that man.

NICKY: Could be.

                      GARY: Could be you're fast.

NICKY: 'Cept I ain't never been in Dodge.

                      MARY: I'm fast enough.

LIZ: Heard tell there was a man in Abilene.

NICKY: Could be.

LIZ: Heard tell he was fast.

NICKY: Could be.

                      GARY: You gonna show me how fast?

NICKY: Course I ain't never been to Abilene.

                      MARY: Why don't you make your play?

LIZ: Could be you was in Wichita.

NICKY: Ain't never been to Wichita.

LIZ: Could be you was in Laramie.

NICKY: Ain't never been to Laramie.

LIZ: Could be you was in Durango, mebbe?

NICKY: Well, mebbe...

                      GARY: You gonna show me how fast?

                      MARY: Why don't you make your play?

LIZ: Or mebbe Cheyenne?

    GARY: You gonna show me?

NICKY: Or mebbe I'm leaving Cheyenne?

    MARY: You gonna make your play?

LIZ: Or mebbe you walked out in the streets of Laredo?

    GARY: You show me.

LIZ: Or mebbe you mebbe you walked out in Laredo one day?

NICKY: Could be.

    MARY: You make your play.

NICKY: 'Cept I never did.

    GARY: Draw!

    MARY: Make me!

    GARY: Yer yeller!

LIZ: Well, I know you from somewhere.

    MARY: Then prove it!

    GARY: You draw!

NICKY: I don't think so.

    MARY: You make me!

LIZ: Sure seems like I seen you before.

    GARY: Yer yeller!

NICKY: I don't think so.

    MARY: You prove it.

LIZ: You sure I don't know you?

NICKY: Yup.

    GARY: And I said: Draw...

LIZ: But I seen you before.

NICKY: No you ain't.

    MARY: And I said: You make me...

LIZ: Sure I have—cause I know you.

NICKY: I don't think so

LIZ: But I seen you.

    GARY: I'm callin ya yeller.

NICKY: Yer wrong.

LIZ: Well, I don't think so.
Think I know you.

                      MARY: Then I dare ya to prove it.

(MARY *falls over dead.*)

                      MARY: And I said: Oh, ya got me, Tex, ya got me bad!

                      GARY: Ya shouldn't a come here, Mister.

                      MARY: And I said: Oh, ya got me, Tex, ya got me bad!

                      GARY: This here's nice quiet town.

                      MARY: And I said: Oh, Tex, I'm gonna bite the dust.

                      GARY: Don't like yer kind round here.

                      MARY: Oh, Tex....

                      GARY: We say: Don't like yer kind round here.
                      Don't like 'em—nope.
                      We say: Don't like yer kind round here.

LIZ: Think I know where I seen you, too...

(ZIVIA *enters doctor's office as* LIZ *exits landscape.*)

                      ZIVIA: Telephone...

NICKY: Mister, you ain't seen me nowhere.

                      ZIVIA: Telephone for Big Dick...
                      Telephone for Mister Big Dick the Sorehead

(GARY *crosses landscape to doctor's office.*)

                      GARY: Yeah, that's me, that's me.

                      ZIVIA: You are Mister Dick?

                      GARY: Just gimme the phone, damn it!

                      ZIVIA: I'll put you through.

(ZIVIA *gives* GARY *the telephone; in the landscape,* NICKY *cradles* MARY *in his arms.*)

MARY: Captain...

NICKY: Yes, Little Bob?

GARY: *(On phone)* Hello?...

MARY: Where are we, Captain?

GARY: Hello? Hello?

MARY: Are we deep beneath the sea?

GARY: Something's wrong with your phone.

ZIVIA: Just a moment, plee-yas...

(ZIVIA *takes telephone back from* GARY.)

NICKY: Yes, Little Bob,
We're very deep.

ZIVIA: *(On phone)* Hello?

NICKY: We're very deep and going deeper.

ZIVIA: *(On phone)* ...Yes?

MARY: How far, how far?

ZIVIA: *(On phone)* Big Dick the Sorehead?...
Well, I'll see...
*(Calls)* Oh, telephone!

NICKY: We're going all the way.

ZIVIA: *(Calls)* Oh, telephone for...

GARY: Gimme that!

NICKY: We're going all the way right down right deep down right to the bottom and back.

GARY: *(On phone)* Hello?

MARY: God willing...

GARY: Hello? Hello?

NICKY: Yes, of course, god willing, Little Bob.

(ZIVIA *takes a second telephone out of her pocket.*)

ZIVIA: *(On phone)* Allo?

GARY: *(On phone)* Hello?

ZIVIA: *(On phone)* Allo?

GARY: *(On phone)* Hello?

ZIVIA: *(On phone)* Who eees dees?

GARY: *(On phone)* This is Big Dick the Sorehead—who is this?

ZIVIA: *(On phone)* Beeg Deek Sorehaid?

GARY: *(On phone)* Yeah—who is this?

ZIVIA: *(On phone)* One moment plee-yas. *(Calls)* Telephone!

GARY: Shut up!

ZIVIA: *(Calls)* Important telephone for Big Dick the Sorehead!

GARY: Take a message!
Could you take a message, please?
Goddamn it, can't you see I'm on the other line?

NICKY: And we shall see what we shall see...

GARY: *(On phone)* Hello?

ZIVIA: *(On phone)* Allo?

GARY: *(On phone)* Hello?

ZIVIA: *(On phone)* Allo?

GARY: *(On phone)* Hello?

ZIVIA: *(On phone)* Who eees dees?

GARY: *(On phone)* This is Big Dick the Sorehead.

ZIVIA: *(On phone)* Beeg Deek Sorehaid?

GARY: *(On phone)* Who the hell is this?

ZIVIA: *(On phone)* One moment plee-yas. *(Calls)* Telephone!

GARY: Goddamn it, take a message!

ZIVIA: Shall I just take a message on that call, Mister Sorehead?

GARY: Can't you see I'm on the other line?

ZIVIA: *(On phone)* I'm sorry, Mister Dickhead is unable to come to the phone right now, babycakes...

MARY: Captain?

NICKY: Yes, Little Bob?

GARY: Who is that?

ZIVIA: *(On phone)* Yes, I'll tell him, honey....

MARY: What shall we see?

    GARY: Who is that? Gimme that! *(On her phone)* Hello....

NICKY: I think the wonders of the deep are what we'll see....

    GARY: Hello? Hello?

NICKY: They will be waiting there for us....

    ZIVIA: She hung up.

    GARY: Did you take a message?

    ZIVIA: Just a moment, plee-yas.

NICKY: That's what I think...

    GARY: Did you take a message?!!

    ZIVIA: *(On her phone)* Mister Sorehead's office...

    GARY: Goddamn it—just take a message!... Hello? Hello? Hello?

MARY: O Captain, do you see that Captain?

    ZIVIA: *(On phone)* ...Heddo?

NICKY: I see them now.

    ZIVIA: *(On phone)* Heddo, prease?

    GARY: *(On phone)* 'Zat-chew, baby?

MARY: O Captain, my hand.

NICKY: I see the wonders of the deep,

    ZIVIA: *(On phone)* Heddo prease?

    GARY: *(On phone)* 'Zat-chew, baby?

MARY: Look, my hand.

NICKY: In fact I see them very clearly now....

    ZIVIA: *(On phone)* I'm sorry—

    GARY: *(On phone)* Hey, 'zat-chew, baby?

MARY: O Captain, my hand is burning.

    ZIVIA: *(On phone)* —your call cannot be completed as dialed...

GARY: *(On phone)* Hey, I'm losing you, baby...

ZIVIA: *(On phone)* If you need assistance...

GARY: *(On phone)* Don't hang up on me, baby!

NICKY: Say your prayers, Little Bob, say your prayers....

GARY: *(On phone)* Please just talk to me, baby, please talk to me...

NICKY: Say your prayers, Little Bob, say your prayers...

*(Fade out)*

END OF PLAY

# CRAZY PLAY #44

# HOW NOT TO GET LAID

## ACT ONE

(GARY *and* ZIVIA *enter the house, she sits on the sofa as* NICKY *and* MARY *enter the doctor's office;* MARY *puts a control device on the desk; they watch the house.*)

GARY: I lost my keys.
Would you believe that—hunh?
Lost my goddamn keys. Just lost 'em. Just like that.
Lemme see that wine list.

You know what I like?
I like that port wine.

See I'm all shitfaced.

                              NICKY: (Wally?)

                                MARY: (Shush)

(MARY *pushes a buzzer on the control device.*)

GARY: I lost my keys, see—
Lost my keys and then I got shitfaced.
Not drunk—I don't get drunk.
I get shitfaced.
You know why?
Hunh?
You know why?

                              NICKY: (This is boring, Wally...)

GARY: You seen my son?

                              MARY: (I don't know—)

GARY: He's a good kid, too but I—
Yeah, he's damn good kid,
But I lost him.

                              MARY: (Maybe it's supposed to be boring.)

GARY: Shit—I lost my fuckin' son.

NICKY: (Wally, nothing's supposed to be
       boring.)

ZIVIA: So what do you want, hunh?
Whaddya have in mind?

GARY: Three guesses.

ZIVIA: Yeah?

GARY: Yeah, wamme ta clue you in?

MARY: (Besides I kinda like it.)

ZIVIA: You looking to party?

NICKY: (You would.)

MARY: (Shush!)

(MARY *pushes a buzzer on the control device.*)

GARY: You got it.

NICKY: (Don't shush me.)

ZIVIA: You like to party?

GARY: Like to party with you.

ZIVIA: Yeah?—

NICKY: (I mean, where do you get off with
       this "shush" crap, anyway?)

ZIVIA: So what's a party, dude?

NICKY: (Man, you are really pushing it!)

ZIVIA: What's a party?

GARY: What do you mean? "What's a party?"

ZIVIA: I'm askin' you what's a party—

NICKY: (You can't tell me to shush!)

ZIVIA: I'm asking what you call a party—

NICKY: (I have as much right to be here as
       you do!)

ZIVIA: You even know what a party is?
I doubt it.

GARY: One way to find out.

ZIVIA: No kidding?

GARY: No kidding.
So you gonna party or you gonna bullshit?

ZIVIA: I don't know.

GARY: That's bullshit.

ZIVIA: No bullshit.
I just don't know about you—

                        NICKY: (Hey, Wally...)

ZIVIA: Just don't know what your scene is, you know—
What gets you off.

                        NICKY: (...Let's make 'em go crazy!)

GARY: Want me to show you?

ZIVIA: Not yet.

                        NICKY: (Come on...)

                        MARY: (No way.)

                        NICKY: (Why not?)

ZIVIA: I'm still trying to make up my little old mind about you.

                        NICKY: (Hunh?)

GARY: Well, don't wait too long.

                        MARY: (Because.)

                        NICKY: (Because you're chicken!)

ZIVIA: Tell you one thing, though—

                        MARY: (I am not.)

                        NICKY: (Chicken.)

ZIVIA: You're really an asshole, aren't you?

GARY: Yeah?

                        MARY: (Okay, but just this once!)

ZIVIA: Well, am I right or am I right?

(MARY *turns the "crazy" dial up all the way;* GARY *grabs* ZIVIA.)

GARY: You fucking bitch, you wanna mess with me....

ZIVIA: Hey, lighten up!

GARY: You lighten up!

                        MARY: (Okay—and that's all!)

(MARY *turns crazy dial back down.*)

ZIVIA: I mean, jeez louise—can't you take a little joke?
Hunh?
Just one little joke.

           NICKY: (You're still a chicken.)

           MARY: (I am not.)

ZIVIA: Heyyyyyy, ass-hole...

GARY: Don't start with that...

           NICKY: (You are so!)

ZIVIA: So we gonna party, or what?

GARY: You tell me.

           MARY: (I don't care, anyway.)

ZIVIA: Okay, let's party.

GARY: Okay.

ZIVIA: So now tell me—
Just what kind of party do you have in mind?

GARY: What do you mean?

ZIVIA: I mean, what kind of party?

GARY: Hey—the regular.

ZIVIA: What's that?

GARY: You know—just the regular.

ZIVIA: What's the regular?

GARY: You know the regular.

ZIVIA: No, I don't know—that's why I'm asking you, okay?
What do you like?

           NICKY: (Oh, boy—is this boring and stupid, or what?)

           MARY: Oh, oh...

ZIVIA: You like two on one?

           MARY: Now look what you did, Gary!!

           NICKY: What?

ZIVIA: You want a little shower?

           MARY: You broke it.

           NICKY: I never touched it!

                                    MARY: Oh, no—it was your idea in the
                                        first place....

ZIVIA: Maybe a little roughhouse?

                                    MARY: It was your idea.

ZIVIA: You tell me.

GARY: Shit...

                                    NICKY: Come on—fix it.

                                    MARY: I don't know how!

                                    NICKY: Well, you could try—you could at
                                        least try!

                                    MARY: I *am* trying....

ZIVIA: You goin' in the back way tonight?

GARY: Hey, cool it, okay—just cool it—what's your scene, anyway—hunh?

                                    NICKY: Cause you're gonna get in trouble
                                        too, you know!

GARY: What's the big deal?

                                    MARY: Not as bad as you.

GARY: I said regular—you know regular?
Regular is regular.
What's the problem?

ZIVIA: No problem.

                                    NICKY: You got it!

                                    MARY: Yeah, but Gary—it won't stabilize.

ZIVIA: I'm just trying to get to know you better.
Know what turns you on.

GARY: You jerkin' me around?

                                    MARY: Oh, nooooooo...

ZIVIA: What do you think?

                                    NICKY: Come on, Wally—you fix it!

                                    MARY: I'm trying!

GARY: Then cut the crap—Listen:
Anything you can get into,
I can get into.

                                    MARY: Oh, noooooooooooo!

ZIVIA: Anything?

GARY: Anything.

(MARY *bangs the control device.*)

                    MARY: Garyyyyyyyyy!

                    NICKY: Whaaaaat?

ZIVIA: Wow, that's great—that's really great.

                    MARY: They're out of control, Gary!
                    Run! Run for your life!

(NICKY *and* MARY *run off downstage right as* LIZ *as "Uncle Fritz" comes around the house, chasing them.*)

ZIVIA: So, listen—you wanna suck cock?

GARY: Hey, you fuckin' listen to me, bitch—

ZIVIA: Grow up, asshole.

GARY: You go fuckin' messin' with me—
I could beat the shit out of you—
Hell, I could fuckin' take you right here right now, and I don't think
    anybody would even give a shit.

ZIVIA: So why don't you?

                    LIZ: Hoo-boy doze kitts iss dryfink me
                        kraaaaaayyyyyyzy!
                    Yost vait'll I get my mitts on 'em—
                    Dell be a spenking dell neffa forget!

(LIZ *exits down right.*)

ZIVIA: No time for a quickie?

GARY: You're fucking sick, you know that?
You're a sick fucking whore.

ZIVIA: Yeah right, I'm a sick fuckin' whore, what does that make you?
Buy me a drink.

GARY: Fuck you.

ZIVIA: I said, buy me a drink.

GARY: And I said fuck you.
Buy it your own fuckin' self.

(MARY *enters up center and runs through the doctor's office, chased by* LIZ *as "Uncle Fritz."*)

                    MARY: Gary, where are you?

LIZ: You krezzzy kitts kom bak!

MARY: Gary—don't leave meeee...

NICKY: *(Off)* Run, Wally!

ZIVIA: Hey, come on—buy me a drink, okay?

(LIZ *enters doctor's office.*)

LIZ: Hoo-boy doze kitts iss dryfink me kraaaaaayyyyyyzy!

ZIVIA: Come on, be nice.

GARY: You are a total fuckin' sicko, you know?

LIZ: *Ach du lieber* dees krezzy kits yost lookit det mess day made mine *gott in himmel— Und meine* machine *kaput! Jahvohl! Dass ist ein fol*-desaster.

ZIVIA: So whaddya really like, hunh?

LIZ: *Aber*—hmmm...

ZIVIA: You wanna tell me?

LIZ: *Ja* vell dis is mebbe not zo bet. Hmf!...

ZIVIA: Wanna try something new?

GARY: Like what?

ZIVIA: Just trust me.

LIZ: I am tinking...mebby I tinker little bit mit dees ting, und...

GARY: Doin' what?

LIZ: ...*(ja, ja, ja)* over here little bit and...

ZIVIA: Hey, try it you'll like it—you remember?

LIZ: ...*ja (das* is not zo *gut* but...)

ZIVIA: "Try it, you'll like it"—Hey, you remember that?

LIZ: Oh vell...
Now, den—vere is dat deGaussing unit?

(LIZ *fixes control device.*)

ZIVIA: "Try it, you'll like it" (Aw, you don't remember....)

LIZ: *Ja*, zo, dass pretty gut, now.

GARY: Lady what is your scene?

ZIVIA: Buy me a drink and I'll clue you in.

*(Fade out)*

## ACT TWO

*(Voices in blackout, singing)*

CHORUS: Don't you go out tonight
Don't you go out tonight
Don't you go o-ver the hill
Don't you go o-ver the hill
Don't you go do what you will
Don't you go do what you will
Don't you go talk-ing all about it
Don't you talk, talk, talk, talk, talk-talk
Don't you talk about it, don't you talk talk talk
You better talk about it
Talk talk talk
You better talk about it
Set-up set-up set-up
Set-up set-up set-up
Set-up...

I saw the man in the air
I saw the man in the air
And he was tum-bl-ing down
He was a tum-bl-ing down
I saw the man in the air
I saw the man in the air
And he was wearing a crown
And he was wearing a crown
You better wind up wind up wind up lemme at it
Better wind up wind up wind up better lemme at it
Catch of the day
Catch of the day

GARY: I ain't no worse than you!

## ACT THREE

*(In the doctor's office, ZIVIA on the telephone; in the house, NICKY and MARY on the sofa)*

        ZIVIA: Can I please just talk to you...?

> ...Well, maybe I do....
>
> ...Cause I need to, okay? Cause I'm trying to understand things.

NICKY: It isn't anything about you, honey...

> ZIVIA: Would you please just talk to me?

NICKY: It isn't anything about you at all—

> ZIVIA: Cause I gotta understand.

NICKY: You just weren't what I wanted—I'm sorry—you know that...

> ZIVIA: But I already said that.

NICKY: You know.

> ZIVIA: I told you that....

NICKY: And I'm sorry, honey, I really am.

MARY: I sure wanted you, baby.

NICKY: I know.

MARY: I wanted you bad.

NICKY: But it just wasn't working, babe.

MARY: I didn't care.

> ZIVIA: Listen, if I thought it would help, I'd say it a hundred times.

MARY: Sometimes in the middle of the night,
When I could feel you, lover—that made me want you so bad.
Other times, when you weren't with me—
Oh I wanted to feel you, darlin', so bad,
And I just didn't care.
You know, I just didn't care.

NICKY: Honey...

MARY: Oh, god I wanted you to want me that way.

NICKY: Hon—I just can't be what you want.

> ZIVIA: ...But I said I'm sorry....

MARY: Yeah sure, babe—tell me about it.

> ZIVIA: ...I said I'm sorry.

MARY: Look, why don't you go—hunh?
Why don't you get the check and go?

        ZIVIA: No, I didn't...I never said that...
        I didn't.
        Don't hang up on me.

MARY: Just tell me what I look like to you, okay?

        ZIVIA: Just don't hang up, you bastard.

MARY: What do I look like to you now? Hunh?
Tell me—go on—be honest.

        ZIVIA: Please, baby, don't hang up on me.

MARY: Go on, be honest.

NICKY: You're a mess, babe.

MARY: Yeah, I'm a mess, thanks a lot.

NICKY: You're all fucked up.

MARY: I know—I'm a mess—I just let myelf go, okay?
And I just don't care.

NICKY: You don't have to do this to yourself.

MARY: What do you care?

NICKY: Why do you do this to yourself?

MARY: You don't care.

NICKY: Why do you treat yourself this way?

MARY: Maybe I'm all fucked up—okay?
Is that okay with you, babe?—Is that okay?

NICKY: Listen to me, okay?

(ZIVIA *has exited office; in the house,* LIZ *in the rear window.*)

        LIZ: But I don't want to make you feel so sad.

NICKY: Just listen to me one time, babe.

        LIZ: And I don't want to make you feel so
           sad and blue, babe, no...

NICKY: It hurts me to see you do this to yourself.

        LIZ: And I don't want to make you sad
           and lonesome, no....
        But I cried a river, darlin'...

MARY: Yeah—I'm all fucked up, hunh?

        LIZ: I cried a river over you.

NICKY: Babe, ya gotta move on...

LIZ: And one of these days, I'm gonna wake
up shining.
And one of these days, I'm gonna lift up my
eyes and go.
And one of these days, I won't feel so sad
and lonesome, honey.
That's all.
That's all....

NICKY: Sometimes ya just gotta move on, babe, believe me.
Sometimes, let's face it—

MARY: What?

LIZ: Look, honey—got your postcard—
Got it all the way down in Mexico.

NICKY: It's for the best.

MARY: Tell me about it.

LIZ: And I don't know why the good Lord
made us this way full of the sadness and
sorrow and suffering that we bring each
other honey, but I'm still here.
Hey, I'm still here.
Hey, I'm still here.

NICKY: Babe, I know what I'm talking about.

LIZ: You gotta help me, operator.
Somebody said it was you but you was gone
when I got there you was gone.
Been gone and travel on for many a mile and
ten.
But I got a soldier boy—and he's a handsome
man,
And bright are his eyes and his hands so soft
and hard and good they feel so good on
me.
They make a mess a ya—what can I say?
What can I say, babe? (Say it ain't workin'.)

MARY: Oh, darling, we could have been so happy.

NICKY: Babe—

LIZ: If you love somebody, shouldn't you
know it?
I mean shouldn't you always know it?
And when you stop loving somebody,

>Oh, baby, shouldn't it make you feel so sad and lonesome?
>And shouldn't you say: Babylove, my babylove,
>Tell me tell me tell me tell me all good children go to heaven.
>Tell me all good children go to heaven.
>And the streets are paved with gold.

NICKY: Ya gotta move on.

LIZ: And Jesus loves me, so they say.

MARY: You bastard...

LIZ: It just gets harder every day.

*(Fade out)*

END OF PLAY

# CRAZY PLAY #31

# NOBODY KNOWS THE (UN-HUNH) TROUBLE I'VE SEEN

## ACT ONE

(ZIVIA *in the doctor's office;* GARY *and* NICKY *as cowboys in the landscape*)

          GARY: Well...

          NICKY: Yup...

          GARY: I love you, Tex.

          NICKY: Yup.

          GARY: 'N I'm yours until the end of time.

ZIVIA: Sheesh—this upset stomach's really getting to me....
I feel...terrible, this gas pain is (whoa!)—
Really making me nauseous—

          NICKY: Well...

          GARY: Yup...

ZIVIA: Musta been something I ate....

          NICKY: I love you back, Tex.

ZIVIA: Sure wish I could just lie down for a second...

          GARY: Yup.

          NICKY: Reckon our love must be a kinda true love.

          GARY: Yup.

          NICKY: Yup.

          GARY: Yup.

          NICKY: Yup.

ZIVIA: Hoo boy—I don't *know*—what the hell did I eat...?

          GARY: But I'm no good for ya, Tex.

          NICKY: Nope.

ZIVIA: Oh Christ—I'm all clammy.

> GARY: I'm...
>
> NICKY: Yer bad, Tex.

ZIVIA: Man, this isn't going away....

> GARY: Yup.
> Cause I'm...
>
> NICKY: You belong to another, Tex

ZIVIA: Oh, that was bad.
That was bad, that was bad—it's really bad.

> GARY: Yup...
>
> NICKY: Yup...
>
> GARY: Yup...

ZIVIA: God—it's bad.

> NICKY: You broke my heart, Tex.

ZIVIA: God—don't let it be a heart attack.

> GARY: Tex, my heart is broke and busted too.

ZIVIA: Oh, God, don't wanna have a heart attack.

> NICKY: Well, you busted mine first, Tex.
>
> GARY: The hell I did.
>
> NICKY: You callin' me a liar?
>
> GARY: I'm callin ya a mangy polecat 'n' a dirty little low-down yellowbellied son of gun and a sidewindin' sodbusting chickenhearted skunk and a liar, Tex.

ZIVIA: Oh man—I feel so bad I feel so bad.

> NICKY: Shouldn't a done that, Tex.
> Shouldn't a made me mad.
> Them's fightin' words...
>
> GARY: Reach!
>
> NICKY: Draw!

ZIVIA: Oh god please help me god please help me god.

(ZIVIA *staggers off right as the telephone on the desk starts to ring;* GARY *falls over and dies.*)

GARY: Oh, Tex, ya got me!...

NICKY: Reckon our love was never meant to be, Tex.

GARY: This is goodbye, Tex... *(Dies)*

NICKY: Yup, but I won't forget you, Tex.

*(Fade out)*


## ACT TWO

*(In the house, LIZ, in an evening gown, stands in the upstage corner.)*

LIZ: Yes. Yes. Yes.
You can hear me now.
Just take a deep breath and let it in and now let it out,
And just let go.
Okay?
Just relax.
Sure.
You can hear me now.
And you can close your eyes.
Okay.
And you can take a deep breath now and let it in and let it out—
Okay.
And you can close your eyes.
And just relax—
Sure, let's relax.
And time and time and time goes by. Okay?
And time and time and time just goes on by, okay?
And now, let's relax.
And now, let's open the door.
And now let's all just open the door.
And just relax, sure.
And just let it come, sure.
And take a good deep breath,
And open the door, and sure, and just a little bit more now,
And come on in—
Okay?
Sure.
And this is the fine time, okay—
This is the very fine time—okay?
And come on in—
Come on in—
Come on in—

Like ya to meet someone.
Sure.
This is my friend.
Okay?
And this is the fine time.
Sure.
And this is my friend.
I'm glad you came.
This is my friend.
I'm glad you came.

*(GARY and MARY in the landscape)*

    MARY: Dad?

    GARY: Shit—where my keys?

    MARY: Can I talk to you, Dad?

    GARY: Where my keys?—God, what if I lost 'em?

    MARY: Maybe you lost 'em, Dad.

    GARY: Oh, god—don't say that, don't say it, don't say it—
    Please, don't just stand there —
    Please, would you look for them, please—
    Would you please just start looking for them, for Chrissake, please instead of standing there like some fucking idiot asshole!

LIZ: Will you answer my questions?
*Okay.*
Tell me your name.
*Okay, my name is...*

    MARY: Dad?

LIZ: *My name is John.*

    MARY: Dad—I'm trying to have a serious conversation!

    GARY: Okay, talk!
    Talk, talk, talk, talk, talk—just help me find 'em, please—help me find em.

LIZ: *John, where you are John?*

    MARY: Dad—didn't you hear me?

LIZ: *Far away I am too far away.*

GARY: Please, please—just help me look!
Don't argue with me—help me look!
Don't just argue.
Can't you look?
Can't you talk and look—see—talk and look—like me?
Shit—why don't you fuckin' goddammit asshole help me find my keys?!

(GARY *breaks down sobbing.*)

LIZ: And is it a fine time, John?
*No. No. Someone is crying.*
Who? John? Can you see?
*Yes, a child a child.*
Yes, can you see John?
*Now now—tower of wind—dog on a beach—rain black rain—*
*A man and a child, a child of woe—*
*Tower of wind on a black beach crying crying crying*
*John the dog.*
*Crying John the dog and raining on the beach.*
*Crying on the beach and the man and the child.*
*And the child of woe,*
*Crying on the beach*

GARY: Oh, God, I'm fucked up, son. I'm so fucked up.

MARY: I'm sorry, Dad.

GARY: Don't talk to me.

MARY: I'm really sorry, Dad.

GARY: Just leave me alone.

MARY: I love you, Dad.

GARY: Oh shut up just shut up with that shit that fucking shit that's shit—you sound like your mother talking—your fucking mother used to talk that kind of shit!

MARY: Don't hit me, dad.
I'll fuckin' take you.

GARY: What?

MARY: Said I'll fucking take you, Dad.
I'll whip your ass.

> GARY: God, you would too wouldn't you oh my god my god that's just the kind of animal you are you'd take your dad and whip his fuckin' ass oh god I'm so ashamed—you'd whip my ass!

LIZ: I am speaking to you now from a center of perfect calm and quiet and understanding.
And ahead of me, as I look, far away in the distance,
A line of clouds.
And beneath the clouds,
The light, which is a perfect light.
And John...

*(The lights start to fade out.)*

> MARY: Dad?

LIZ: John the dog...

> GARY: DON'T TALK TO ME!
> I'M MORTIFIED.

LIZ: John the dog is crying.

*(Fade out)*


## ACT THREE

*(NICKY down center talking to audience)*

NICKY: And people say to me, Jerry—
How can I change my life right now?
How can I start up that stairway to success?
Because they've seen the people do it, like we show you—
Ordinary men and women from every walk of life—
People like yourselves—
They say to me: Jerry—what's the secret?
And I tell 'em: The secret is the knowledge.

And they say: But, Jerry, what is this knowledge and isn't it hard to find it, and hard to use it and I say:
If you knew what every successful person knows,
You'd know how simple it really is....

And I just wish I had the time to talk to each and every one of you individually, and show you how simple it really is to change your life completely and join the hundreds and thousands and millions of successful men and women all around the world—
Because you are supposed to be successful—don't you know that?

Sure you do—
You are supposed to be a success in life—you know that—
But you just don't know how to do it and it's as simple as that.

So when people say to me: Jerry, but don't I need a special skill or a talent or an attitude...?
Friends, the only attitude you have to have is the desire to change your life right now—
Because it's up to you,

You have to want that change—

You must desire that change with all your heart and mind and soul and not only that—
You must be prepared to make that change right now.
And those of you that have this desire—you already know that the only other thing you need is the knowledge and once you get that knowledge, you're gonna put it to work right now,
And that's why we talk about changing your life right now.

But you have to reach out, you have to call—I can't call you—
And so many of you now will take down the number I'm gonna give you and put it aside and that's a pity really,
Because this is knowledge that was meant for you to have—

You are supposed to have this knowledge.

And let me just promise you—and friends I can make this promise because I have seen it work time after time after time in Mississippi and
Massachusetts and South Dakota, North Dakota, North Carolina, New York City—
If you put this knowledge to work for you tomorrow morning,
I promise you will see the results tomorrow night,

Friends, the lines are open, operators are standing by, but I can't call you, you have to make that call.
And I promise if you make that call right now,
Just pick up the phone, wherever you are—and there is a telephone within a hundred yards of you no matter where you are—call me right now and I promise you, I really do, this time next week, one week from today, you'll be saying Jerry I can't believe how my life has changed because I am walking up that highway to happiness and climbing my own personal stairway to success.

Thank you all and God bless.

*(Fade out)*

## ACT FOUR

*(In the landscape:* GARY *on the ground,* MARY *as a cowboy watching;* ZIVIA *in the doctor's office:* LIZ *in the house on sofa)*

    GARY: ....creamy thighs and oh her tender breasts like rosebuds
    Yes and down I would go and up she came and hair like the
    Oh let's say the whinnying steed but dreamy thighs
    She had thighs my God like cocoa butter, Doctor
    Just like ice cream on a stick it was so thick and runny for me then!

    MARY: I'm aimin' ta shoot ya, Mister!

    GARY: And I had other thoughts I had my own ideas.

    MARY: I'm aimin' ta shoot ya down in the cold blood, like ya shot my Paw.

    GARY: But why?

ZIVIA: *(On phone)* I'll hold.

    GARY: Oh, why? Can't you see? She was the darkling beauty of my days then I like a Mormon like a madman took that mermaid for her thighs like butterfat and nipples like the boisenberry in a snowbank
    And down I would go and up she came
    And down I would go and up she came just like the rocking horse...

ZIVIA: *(On phone)* I'll keep holding.

    GARY: She took the bit between her tiny teeth and showed it to me 'cause I saw it there I saw it sparkle yes and she said how she fancied an affair and we kept waltzing on forever on my rocking horse.

    MARY: Ya ready to die?

ZIVIA: *(On phone)* Hello?

GARY: Oh, Doctor, I don't want to die....

(NICKY *enters landscape.*)

LIZ: Say hello...

NICKY: You gonna shoot-shoot, sonny?
Gonna click-it?
Well, go on, then.

MARY: I ain't got no reason to hear you!
I ain't got no call to care.
I ain't got no time for the wasting.
I gotta fire in the hole.

ZIVIA: *(On phone)* Hello?

NICKY: Hello?

LIZ: Say hello...

MARY: I ain't got no reason god help me to walk this earth!

ZIVIA: *(On phone)* Yes, I'll hold.

NICKY: Dad?

GARY: Shut up.

NICKY: Please don't die on me, Dad.

ZIVIA: *(On phone)* ...I'm holding....

NICKY: Dad?

GARY: Just leave me alone.

(GARY *gets up and confronts* NICKY.)

NICKY: Please don't die on me, Dad.

GARY: Shut up.

ZIVIA: *(On phone)* ...Hello?...

GARY: I never liked you.
I never did.
And you were a piss poor kid, you were a shitty kid you were the worst!

NICKY: Please don't die on me, dad.

MARY: Oh Paw jes lookit me lookit me lookit me lookit me crine for ya, Paw—
I'm sad and crine for ya, Paw—
I'm jest sending mah tears on down to find

                    you,
                    Jest sendin' em down...

ZIVIA: *(On phone)* I'm holding....

                    NICKY: Dad...?

ZIVIA: *(On phone)* Hello...

                    NICKY: Does it hurt?

                    MARY: Oh, Paw.

                    GARY: Click, bang, yer daid, stranger.

                    MARY: Pawwwwwwww...

(MARY *dies.*)

ZIVIA: *(On phone)* Hello? Hello?

LIZ: Say hello...

                    GARY: Run ya little bare butt—run till I
                    catch ya!

ZIVIA: *(On phone)* Hello?

LIZ: Say hello...

And we say everybody need somebody sometime
Say it again
And we say everybody need somebody sometime
Say it again
And we say everybody need somebody sometime
Say it again
And we say come on come on up to Kool
And we say come on come on up to Kool
And we say come on come on up to Kool
And we say oh what a friend we have in thank you Jesus
Just say it again
And we say oh what a friend we have in thank you Jesus
Just say it again
And we say oh what a friend we have in thank you Jesus
Just say it again

| | |
|---|---|
| Just say it again | (MARY *starts to sing*) |
| Say it again. | MARY: And we were sail-ing, |
| Say it again | Across the sea.... |
| Just say it again | And we were sail-ing, |
| Say it again | Across the sea.... |
| Say it again | And we were sail-ing, |
| Bye now | Across the sea.... |
| Bye now | And we were sail-ing, |

Say it again  
Bye now  
You'll be sorry  
Say it again.  
Bye now  
And you'll be sorry  
Just say it again.  
And we say somebody left the  
    cake out in the shoop shoop  
We say shoop-shoop.  
And we say sha-la-la-laliday  
And we say sha-la-la-laliday  
    life is a holiday  
And we say it again  
And we say sha-la-la-la-liday,  
    life is a holiday  
And we say bye now  
Bye now  

We say bye now  

Across the sea....  
And we were sail-ing,  
Across the sea....  
And we were sail-ing,  
Across the sea....  
And we were sail-ing,  
Across the sea....  
And we were sail-ing,  

Across the sea....  
And we were sail-ing,  
Across the sea....  

And we were sail-ing,  
Across the sea....  

And we were sail-ing,  
Across the sea....  
And we were sail-ing,  
Across the sea....  
And we were sail-ing,  
Across the sea....  

*(Fade out)*

## END OF PLAY

# ABOUT THE CRAZY PLAYS—AN AFTERWORD

THE CRAZY PLAYS represent the culmination of a seven-year exploration of collage writing techniques. Originally, my impulse had been to circumvent the tyranny of style. If drama is in some rightful sense about other people but the author creates all the characters, how is it possible to introduce voices which aren't in the final analysis simply one's own? Reading more or less whatever came to hand, I copied sentences and paragraphs that caught my interest, without regard to how they might be used in a play or, indeed, whether they were even in dialog form or inherently dramatic. Then, having amassed a substantial number of excerpts from sources as varied as Gilgamesh, THE IMPORTANCE OF BEING EARNEST, junk mail solicitations and B-movie scripts, I began to try cutting them up and sticking them back together to make scenes.

It was obvious from the start that words became effective to the extent that they seemed to stand in some sort of relationship to an action. I began to think of collage as an inversion of the conventional writing process, and by taking the words as a given and working back to the situation, it seemed possible to treat the choice of action as an abstract or formal question instead of a matter of meaning or content. Of course, the relation between words and action seemed far less precise, far more contingent than in the usual play, but any incongruity between word and deed texts generally had the effect of making the action seem more autonomous, ambiguous, even dreamlike. I became aware of ways in which the style and content of certain texts—say, the balcony scene from ROMEO AND JULIET—carried associations with them and created "historical" contexts despite even radical editing. Finally, I began to realize that on every level of the process—from selecting the words to assembling the situations to editing those into the play itself—my choices were necessarily deeply personal, reflecting my deepest assumptions about the nature of the world and human beings.

Between 1983 and 1989 I created and staged a cycle of three plays—DER INKA VON PERU, TOMORROWLAND and WIPEOUT—in which I set out to use found texts from a specific cultural epoch (e.g., Classical Antiquity or the Cold War) to express the basic narratives by which we "understood" these epochs. Quite by accident, I also began to direct actors for the first time, and realized that they too found it essential to invent narratives for their characters—narratives which, I hasten to add, didn't need to be identical with the narratives I had invented in writing or, one suspects, with the narratives audiences would eventually perceive. But if communication—from writer to actor and actor to audience—could still prevail despite so many misunderstandings, then the de-constructionists are right. Reading a work of art is always in essence a reading-in, and we maintain coherence in our world (and art) by passing around and sharing the same basic narrative "lenses."

If this were true, I thought, then it ought to be possible for me to get at my own obesssions by various associative processes (such as automatic writing) and collage the resultant texts into plays which audiences would find reflective of their own obsessions, too (without, you see, my necessarily having to know what those were)—in other words, a kind of linguistic abstract expressionism. THE CRAZY PLAYS are the result, and assonance aside, I call them "Crazy" first to suggest that they make "no sense"; then to suggest that they do in fact express unconscious, obsessive, even "dark" psychological states; and finally, echoing the traditional "crazy quilts", to suggest that this way of looking at things is bred in the American bone.

*Brooklyn, New York*
*June 1992*

# THE ENDLESS ADVENTURES OF M C KAT OR HOW THEY GOT FROM A TO B

## CRAZY PLAY NUMBER 51

THE ENDLESS ADVENTURES OF M C KAT was written during a residency at the MacDowell Colony in January/February 1991 and first presented in April 1991 by Cucaracha Theater at the Broome Street Theater in New York. The cast and creative contributors were:

| | |
|---|---|
| TEX | Cheryl Scaccio |
| MONICA SCOTT, M D | Liz Schofield |
| M C KAT | Zivia Flomenhaft |
| RICHARD SOREHEAD | Damian Young |
| BOB HOWARD | Mark Dillahunt |
| GARY COHEN | Hugh Palmer |
| BAD TEX | Jamie Richards |
| OG OGGLEBY | Michael Bubrick |
| CITIZENS OF THE MIDDLE OF NOWHERE | Al Cima |
| THE LONESOME POKE | Mollie O'Mara |

| | |
|---|---|
| *Director, designer & score* | Jeffrey M Jones |
| *Lights* | Ken Posner |
| *Costumes* | Lizzie Gulczynski |
| *Stage management* | Aaron Singer |

In production, the character of M C KAT was performed by Zivia Flomenhaft manipulating a small stuffed animal. The various CITIZENS were performed by Al Cima with minor costume changes. The action was accompanied by a continuous, multi-track tape-loop score.

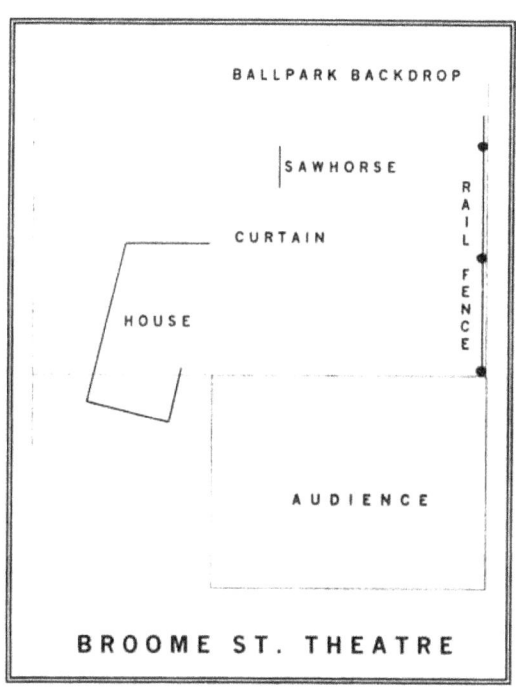

# AN EXPLANATION

Given the acclaim that has attended the meteoric rise of M C Kat, it may seem churlish to remind the reader that he is not only hairy and extremely short (twelve inches high in stocking feet) but, in fact, neither human nor even alive. Whether this makes him the latest in the long line of animated creatures to achieve artistic immortality or just another "stuffed" (to use the schoolyard slur) animal depends, in the last analysis, upon one's liberality of mind. Whatever the case, it is important to note that Mister Kat is always accompanied in his public appearances by a human being, and that this person is not only considered a full and equal collaborator in his work but, in every instance, a union member compensated at an appropriate level.

—The Author

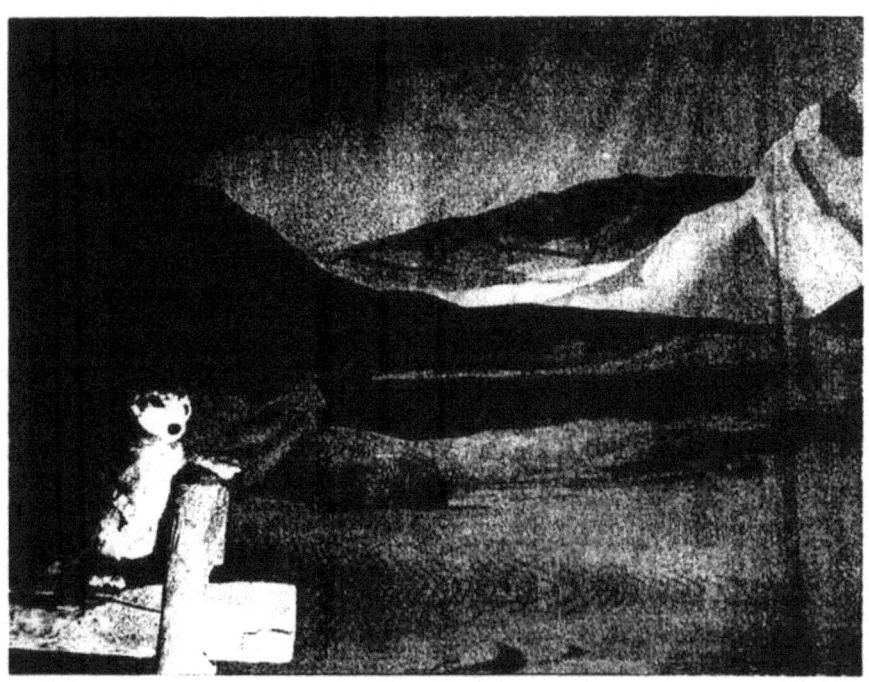

# ACT ONE

(TEX *on fence;* DICK *and* M C *in house, sitting in window*)

TEX: And now, folks...time fer "Stress and Health"
Yer guide to stress and health,
By Monica Scott, M D
A singin' ti-yi-yippie-yippie-yay yippie-yay
A singin' ti-yi-yippie-yippie-yay...

So long.

(MONICA *enters center from behind curtain as* TEX *exits up.*)

MONICA: As a doctor,
It's my job to provide busy men and women like yourselves with medical information which, hopefully,
You can "take to the bank."
I'm Monica Scott—and thank you for joining me as we look at stress.
Because whether or not we may understand why,
Research has shown that stress not only causes cancer
But the more severe cancers—
This was discovered actually through research with different animals because, as you probably know, animals find different things stressful.
For example, hoofed animals, such as horses, cows and goats, etc., can become profoundly stressed by cattle guards or even lines on the pavement, whereas other animals such as rodents are not bothered by lines on the pavement at all.

M C: Hey!

MONICA: One thing that does stress a rodent, though, is being spun around.

M C: Hey, where am I?

DICK: Shhhhhhhhhh.

MONICA: For example, living in a cage where the bottom turns around like a record player.

DICK: You're right here, M C.

M C: Oh...

MONICA: In fact, a rat raised in an environment where he is spun around all the time will develop cancer.
And this happens not just to the occasional rat, but to all rats. So—

M C: So, what's going on?...

MONICA: Can stress cause cancer in humans just like in rats?

DICK: Shhhhhh...

MONICA: The answer is "yes."

DICK: Not much....

MONICA: Here's another example: Baboons—
Baboons mate for their entire lifetime with the same baboon;
So, separate a baboon couple, placing the female in a glass cage with the male in another glass cage right beside her, then put a second male into the cage with the female—they now become a new couple—
And if the original male is forced to keep watching,
He will develop a terminal illness and die.
Of course, there are many many other examples
If a rat's feet are tied together, for example,

M C: Hey!

MONICA: They develop tumors.

M C: Hey, where am I?

DICK: You're right here, damn it, now settle down.

M C: Oh...

MONICA: If a monkey is required to push a lever to prevent another monkey from receiving an electric shock,
This monkey will also develop a tumor from the stress, which is known as the "Brady effect" or the "executive monkey" phenomenon.

M C: I thought I got lost.

DICK: You didn't get lost.

M C: Whew!

MONICA: Uh—poisoning accidents in preschool-aged children—

M C: That was a close one!

MONICA: Another thing that can be stress-related—

M C: Yay for MEEEEEEEEE!!!!

DICK: Shhhhhhhh!!!!!

MONICA: Talking now about children involved in repeat poisoning accidents, kids consuming things like whole bottles of drain cleaner time after time—because in fact,

*(Enter BOB HOWARD around curtain, center.)*

BOB: Hello...

MONICA: The recurrence rate for poisoning accidents in preschool-age children is a hundred-twenty-five times greater than chance so uh...

BOB: Just me again...

MONICA: These are exposures that really couldn't be considered "accidents" at all.

BOB: And welcome to Bob Howard's World of Love...
Tonight, I'm feeling in a mood—
Let's say, impulsive...

MONICA: Research indicates that poisoning accidents in preschool-age children have nothing to do with storage in the home,

BOB: But can I trust you with my secrets?

MONICA: Nothing to do with information about toxic substances—

BOB: I don't think so....
*(He exits up center.)*

MONICA: It has to do with stress!
So the jury is in:
Stress equals death!
Now, let's take another example.

*(Exit MONICA stage right: DICK and M C in house)*

DICK: I don't know what's the matter—
I'm just not myself—
You know what I mean?
I'm just not myself.
You know what I mean?
I'm just not myself.

M C: Aw, shut up ya big galoot!

DICK: You know what I mean—
I mean, even the meerkat was starting to bug me.

M C: That's me—M C Kat!

DICK: I mean, something's wrong....

M C: Get it—M C—Meer Cat?

DICK: Maybe it's the weather...

M C: Yay for MEEEEEE!

Dick: ...Maybe it's me, maybe it's not me—
Maybe it's the fact I'm cooped up inside here trying to write this stupid-ass play and it's all just pure crap!

M C: With a big part for me in it.

Dick: With a big part for you in it.

M C: Yeah, I'm the star!

Dick: I dunno, something's wrong, I dunno,
Something's wrong, I dunno,
Something's wrong, I dunno,
I'm just not myself.

M C: Aw shut up ya big galoot.

Dick: You know what I mean?
I mean I'm just stuck in this goddamn endless loop of misery and pain, I dunno maybe it's midlife crisis I dunno vitamin deficiency, I dunno, the beginning of the end, something, maybe it's my goddamn sinus problem who cares you don't care I don't care but I'm telling you man I just feel bad real bad real down I feel real down I just feel terrible....

(Enter MONICA D S R, around house)

Monica: Now, for years doctors thought there were two kinds of anger—the anger held-in and the anger expressed outwardly—and that only the anger held-in could cause problems.
Well, unfortunately, we now know all anger is dangerous,

M C: Hey!

Monica: And that means managing anger—

M C: Hey, where am I!

Monica: Using, for example, techniques such as these developed by Duke Williams,
The leading authority on anger control—

M C: Hey, I'm talking to you, ya big galoot!

Dick: Aw, shut up, M C—you're right here!

Monica: Carry a little pocket notebook—

M C: Peckerhead!

Monica: Your hostility log.

Dick: Look, I'm just not myself.

MONICA: Whenever you realize you're thinking cynical thoughts, make an entry—if you're around other people, do it later, but don't put it off—
And every entry should include the time and place, who did what, actual thoughts that went through your head, any emotions you felt and any action you took.

M C: So, what's going on?

MONICA: Typical page might look something like this:

DICK: Just cool it, ok?

*(Enter BOB around curtain, center)*

MONICA: Tuesday, 12/20, 1:15 P M: In car—driving—young man, probably a teenager, raced past me, cut me off—
Thoughts:

BOB: I'm back....

MONICA: Damn teenage driver!

BOB: And baby, I'm trouble....

MONICA: Feelings:

BOB: Yes—

MONICA: Irritation, urge to kill.

BOB: So many hiding places in my World of Love.

MONICA: Actions:

BOB: Which one do you like best?

MONICA: Gave him a mean look.
Now stop those angry thoughts!
How?

BOB: You think nobody knows.

MONICA: Simply tell them.

BOB: But it's so obvious....

MONICA: As soon as you're having those angry thoughts, just yell loud as you can,
"STOP!"

BOB: Come on, girl...

MONICA: Surprisingly, those thoughts will actually stop.

BOB: Let's go...

MONICA: Go ahead, yell out loud, at the top of your lungs—

BOB: You know what I want?

MONICA: "STOP!"

BOB: I want to give you that thrill, girl—

MONICA: Okay, then reason with yourself.
You are a rational person—
Go ahead—

BOB: You know,

MONICA: Reason with yourself.

BOB: That thrill you need...

MONICA: Begin a speech to yourself that goes something like this:

BOB: You're gonna let me, aren't you?

MONICA: "Lighten up!

BOB: And I'm gonna like it.

MONICA: You know gosh darn well that punk didn't get out of bed this morning saying to himself, "Hey, man, old (and here you use your own name)".

BOB: Make me...

MONICA: "Bet old what's-his-name is gonna try to deposit that check down at the bank today."

BOB: Make me beg.

MONICA: "Heh-heh-heh—"

BOB: Cause you know you can....

MONICA: "Guess I'll just get into my car, and drive right in front of him and cut him off!"

BOB: Are you afraid...?

MONICA: So learn to be philosophical.

BOB: What if I'm frightened also?

MONICA: And laugh at yourself.

BOB: What if I need to trust you with my shame?

MONICA: If you don't, believe me, other people will.

BOB: What if that's just what turns me on the most?

(*Exit* MONICA *down stage right, followed by* BOB.)

DICK: Oh, I don't know, I don't know, I don't know, I don't know, I don't know what's the matter....

M C: Aw, shut up about it will ya yer driving me crazy!

DICK: I'm just not myself.

(GARY COHEN *enters house and sits down in window.*)

GARY: And hello again everybody....

DICK: So I turn on the radio, okay?

GARY: From Shea Stadium...

DICK: Even the radio's bringing me down...

GARY: Gary Cohen, once again without Bob Murphy,
Inviting you to join us for another evening of Post-Season Baseball brought to you once again by Digestin....
When you need major league relief—
Send for Digestin.

(*Enter* TEX *from behind curtain, center*)

TEX: Now folks, at this time
And on the advice of counsel,
The management of this-here thee-ater and the producers of this-here play would like to make the following disclaimer,
Which shall be known forevermore herein as the "Disclaimer" and it goes like this:
To wit, that the character of one so-called Mister Gary Cohen,
Who is referred to in the play as the radio announcer for the New York Mets,
Ain't actually to be confused with any real Gary Cohen, who might be living or dead, or might or might not be some kind of actual radio-type of announcer for the New York Mets or even some other baseball franchise;

(*Enter* BAD TEX, *up center*)

BAD TEX: Don't I know you?

TEX: I don't think so.
Two—
That the so-called character of this-here M C Kat,

M C: H'ray for MEEEEEEE!

TEX: Who is referred to in the play as a stuffed animal...

M C: Uhhhhhh—wait a minute...

TEX: Ain't to be confused with any animal stuffed er otherwise...

M C: Who you calling stuffed!

TEX: Er living er dead er made up er....

M C: I am not a stuffed animal, I'm an animated creature.

TEX: So on and so forth...

BAD TEX: Sure I know you—

TEX: No, I don't think so.
And third—that this-here so-called character of Richard Sorehead...

M C: Hey—you gonna let him get away with that...

TEX: Alias Dick the Sorehead,

DICK: Shut up, M C!

TEX: Alias Big Dick Sorehead and/or Big Dick the Sorehead,

M C: Weenie...

TEX: Why he ain't to be confused with any actual sorehead, folks,

DICK: You call me that again, I'll bop you!

TEX: Nor nobody actual, come to think of it, no matter if they's living or dead or made up or not made up er—
Shoot, folks—there ain't nothing in this play at all that's supposed to be confused with anything that ever was or is or will be now or any other time right here or any other place in perpetuity throughout the universe world without end...

BAD TEX: Yer that sissy, ain't ya.

TEX: ('Scuze me, folks)
Now Mister—them's fighting words.

M C: Ahhhh—yer a weenie you can't even stand up for yourself you just sit there feeling sorry for yourself all day—what a wimp!

BAD TEX: You gonna back that up?

DICK: You wanna get dry-cleaned?

M C: No.

DICK: Then clean up your act.

TEX: I'd like to see you make me.

M C: Okay...

BAD TEX: Reach!

TEX: Awwwwww—
Ya got me Tex, ya got me bad.

M C: Folks, we're a poor theater....

BAD TEX: Yup, looks bad...

M C: And we worked hard to get this show up....

BAD TEX: Looks like a gut shot, Tex.

M C: Going without pay,

TEX: Yup, it was a gut shot, Tex.

M C: Day after day...

BAD TEX: That's bad.

TEX: Real bad, real real real bad....

M C: All of us chasing what I like to call the elusive butterfly of personal fulfillment....

TEX: Oh, Tex...

BAD TEX: What?

TEX: Tex...

M C: So please don't sue us, folks!

BAD TEX: What?

TEX: I'm gonna bite the dust....

M C: Cause we're good people.

BAD TEX: Well, so long, cowboy...

M C: Except for (you know) maybe one or two not so good.

TEX: And tell 'em I died with my boots on.

(TEX *staggers off behind curtain, followed by* BAD TEX.)

DICK: So I've got the *radio* on, okay?

GARY: And hello again, everybody...

M C: So how was I?

DICK: Nauseating.

GARY: From Shea Stadium,
Gary Cohen once again with*out* Bob Murphy

M C: Yer just jealous....

DICK: Radio's bringing me *down*....

GARY: Inviting you to join us for another evening of Post Season Baseball;
Bob Murphy of course still taking that well-earned Caribbean cruise vacation
Because the Mets not actually scheduled to play here for several more months yet...
So with a light snow falling and a wind-chill factor of minus ten degrees
No action visible of any kind at Shea—
And the field just plunged in darkness.
And since there's a lull in the action,

Let's turn now to our first guest in the broadcast booth,
Richard Sorehead, better known I guess to his one or two friends as Big Dick—did I get that right, Big Dick?

DICK: Yeah, Big Dick Sorehead actually...

GARY: Hey, well glad to have you on board, Dick,
What's going on?

DICK: Well, I don't know Gary, I'd have to say I just don't know—
Possibility that I'm not myself.

GARY: Know what you mean, Dick Sorehead,
And I'm sure the entire broadcast staff joins with me in wishing you a speedy recovery.
But in a situation like this where you know something's wrong, seems to me you always have to ask the question is it a mental attitude type of deal, is there the possibility of an injury involved, and what about the stress factor?

DICK: Yeah, well I don't know, Gary,
Maybe bad attitude on my part,
Maybe some kind of drug and alcohol problem—
Maybe the fact that I'm always surrounded by *fatheads*—

M C: Aw, shut up ya big galoot!

DICK: YOU TELL ME, OKAY?

GARY: Okay...
Little emotional outburst here in broadcast booth folks and we do apologize...
Of course stress build-up part of the post season
And we do want to bring you the whole story—raw, and uncensored though it may be...

M C: So who's this guy?

DICK: Some asshole...

GARY: Uh, we're on the air, Dick.

DICK: Okay, "bozo"—you like that word better, asshole?

GARY: Just informed Dick Sorehead called away on business folks so we'll be getting to that interview some other time...
Which leaves us with...oh...I'd say about four and half more hours to kill thanks to the toilet-mouth of someone I could mention...

M C: Interview me.

GARY: Baseball of course not merely a game of inches but sometimes a game of hours...

M C: Hey, interview me...

GARY: Remember once when I was still in high school
Broadcasting the play by play for the kumquat league over my granddad's crystal set...
Nothing much ever happened,
But I did want to share that memory with you folks...
The time just hangin' kinda heavy on the hands here now....

M C: Hi.

GARY: How ya doin?

M C: Uhhhhh—I knew Bob Ruth, you know.

GARY: Beg your pardon?

M C: You know—Bob Ruth, the Sultan of Swat?

GARY: Uh, no, that's Babe Ruth.

M C: Oh—well, you could interview me anyway.
You know—ask me questions and stuff.

GARY: You know, folks...

M C: I mean, seeing as how I've got a featured role in an important New York production....

GARY: Sometimes here in the broadcast booth late at night the mind does play tricks on a fellow...

M C: I mean, it's not like I made it up—ask him...

GARY: *Animal* talking to me now...

M C: Yeah, M C Kat, I'm the star of the show.

GARY: What appears to be a furry, golly—ten, twelve-inch high little sucker...

DICK: It's called a meerkat, Gary...

GARY: Wanna say prairie dog...

M C: No, meerkat—meeeer-kat, got it?

DICK: Meerkats being the small gregarious burrowing animal from southern Africa that's related to the mongoose, Gary.

GARY: Stand corrected on that...

DICK: Natural enemies include those carrion birds.

M C: Yuck, carrion birds—I hate 'em!

GARY: Well, thank you, Dick.

DICK: You're welcome, Gary.

M C: Yeah, so now let's talk about me!
Yay for MEEEEEEEEE!

DICK: Cool it!

M C: Sorry, I got carried away.
Okay, I'm ready for the interview now,
Ask me anything—ask me about current events, I'm well informed....

GARY: Well, as it happens I do have a copy of the paper *(N Y Post)* with me, and I was wondering if maybe I could get your reaction to the headline... *(Reads today's headline)*

M C: Well, I was shocked, Gary.

GARY: Un-hunh...

M C: Shocked, saddened, saddened and shocked—
You know, first I was saddened, then I was shocked.
In fact, I'm in still in shock, I really can't talk about it, sorry.

GARY: Just a follow-up on that...

M C: No Gary, I'm sorry, but I don't think first amendment guarantees justify that kind of invasion of privacy.

GARY: Constitutional issues there, of course, and we'll be getting into that on the wrap-up, but if I could just get you back to baseball for a minute, little fella...

M C: Yeah, I play baseball—
Meerkat league.

GARY: Didn't even know they had that actually....

M C: Yeah, I'm the star.

DICK: (It's softball, Gary...)

GARY: (Thank you, Dick...)
And just exactly what position do you play, M C?

M C: Oh, I play 'em all!

GARY: Plays 'em all—

DICK: (Slowpitch softball...)

GARY: Any particular favorites?

M C: Well, I guess I like running back the best.

DICK: (Girl's intramural slowpitch softball, Gary.)

M C: No, it's not, you big galoot!

GARY: Talking with the meerkat here, folks.

DICK: And Gary?

GARY: What?

DICK: Notice anything wrong, Gary?

GARY: Gee, I...

DICK: That's right Gary—you're interviewing a stuffed animal.

M C: DON'T CALL ME THAT!

DICK: Oh, god...

M C: Don't call me a stuffed animal!

DICK: I'm sorry, M C, I'm sorry, I'm sorry, I'm sorry....

M C: Not a stuffed animal!

DICK: Just slipped out.

M C: I'm an animated creature and you know it!

DICK: It just slipped out...

M C: You're not sorry...

DICK: Yes I am...

M C: No, you're not.

DICK: I am so!

M C: Go away.

DICK: M C, please—it just slipped out!
Honest—okay?

M C: Yeah, well...

DICK: I promise—I'll never say it again....

M C: Maybe if you buy me something...

GARY: Touching...real-life drama going on here, folks—
Gonna try to get a microphone in there—see if we can do this...

DICK: Uh, no that's okay, Gary, no need to sneak around.

GARY: Okay, well—Geez—amazing real-life situation captured here, guys—
Any thoughts, any reactions?

DICK: Well I, I made a mistake, Gary,
I don't think we need to dwell on it...

GARY: Just would like to go into that mistake though if I could, Dick.

DICK: Look, I used a slur in a moment of thoughtlessness, okay?
And I just...feel terrible now....

GARY: Big Dick maybe learning an important lesson here.
And if I may just add a personal note:
To those who say that Baseball's just a game,
I say: look deeper—
Look where it starts,
Springing up on sand lots in the tenements,
On fields of dreams between the Indiana cornrows
Do you see the children playing there?
Learning, like dad before 'em,
Teamwork and good sportsmanship?
But there's a darker side to this great game—

DICK: O K...I think we're heard just about enough of this....

GARY: The side of bigotry and—Dick...
And hatred—please don't do it, Dick...
And slurs—don't turn me off, Dick, please don't turn me off.
*(Weeping)* Don't wanna go away...

M C: Now look what you did.

GARY: Please don't make me go away—

DICK: Oh, shut up!

GARY: I'm so lonely...

(DICK *and* M C *watch* GARY *slide down below the window sill as* MONICA *enters D S R, in front of house.*)

MONICA: Do you feel our world is a good place or a bad place?

DICK: Not my goddamn fault...

M C: Yeah it is.

MONICA: If there are setbacks, is it always your fault?

DICK: No, it's not!

M C: Yup-yup, yup, yup...

MONICA: Research demonstrates your feelings about these questions can be changed.
Which reminds me of an experience I had as a teenager:

(M C *follows* GARY *as* OG OGGLEBY *appears outside house, in upstage window.*)

OG: Excuse me, sir...

MONICA: As a high school student,
I began dating a boy whose family was very involved with the church.

OG: Sir?

MONICA: They only allowed him to go out twice a week,
And even then they made him come home early.

OG: I know you're in there, sir.

DICK: Go away!

MONICA: So I started going to church just to be with him.

OG: I'd like to take a moment of your time to talk about the Lord, sir.

DICK: Fuck off!

MONICA: Now the church had an unusual minister.

OG: Did you know God is love, sir?

MONICA: If I were to diagnose him today,
I would describe him as a limited individual with obsessive tendencies.
Because very single Sunday, he gave the same piece of advice:

OG: Have a nice day, sir.

(*Exit* OG; *enter* BOB HOWARD *D S R as* MONICA *crosses center*)

MONICA: If he didn't preach a whole sermon on the topic he'd "sneak it in"
to a sermon on anything else:
And his point was that in solving problems you should simply ask,

BOB: My name is Bob and....

MONICA: "What would Jesus do?"

BOB: ...and I'm illiterate....

MONICA: And the idea was what if you did what Jesus would have done...
Everything would work out fine.

BOB: Don't even got no underwear or nothin' cause I just don't know no better.
But I got feelings...

MONICA: Now, it may have been due to the fact that I was a budding scientist at the time,
But I decided to try an experiment to see if it worked.

BOB: Yeah, I can be hurt...

MONICA: So, as I encountered my little teenage problems...

BOB: Real bad....

MONICA: (And as a matter of fact, just between you and me, my not so little teenage problems)...

BOB: So please don't hurt me baby....

MONICA: I would ask myself,

BOB: 'Cause I think you could....

MONICA: "What would Jesus have done?"
Well, after a few weeks of this, I began to realize that Jesus would never have gotten himself into my predicaments in the first place!"

BOB: See—I can't express myself too good in words...

MONICA: I mean—

BOB: I'm better with my hands when I get physical.

MONICA: Can you imagine the man you read about in Matthew, Mark, Luke and John allowing the situation to deteriorate to the point where he's dealing with the kind of stuff you and I have to deal with?

BOB: Sometimes I like to sit out in my car in the middle of nowhere and just howl
And then I drive real fast, like I don't care or nothin'—

MONICA: Or to put it another way,

BOB: It's scary as hell, but it's just the way I am.

MONICA: Scientific research confirms that the best way to deal with stress is simply to avoid it in the first place.

BOB: Long as I can remember, folks said I was no good...
...just kinda hunky...

MONICA: So what about situations where nothing can be done?

BOB: And I'm still no good, but woman, I'm hot for you.

MONICA: Best advice a doctor can give:

BOB: I'm hot, and I'm trashy—Hell...

MONICA: Be philosophical!

BOB: You're gonna love it.

(MONICA *and* BOB *exit up center;* OG *enters D S R around house, looking in through front window.*)

OG: Excuse me, sir, I'd like to talk about the Lord, have you been saved? You know that Jesus...
(Oh, I'm sorry, that's supposed to be a question)
Did you know Jesus Christ is coming soon to...
(Wait a minute, skipped some stuff)
ARMAGEDDON, what does that it mean to you?
Did you know Armageddon was a proven scriptual I mean scriptrural I mean scriptrurial...

(DICK *stands, walks over to* OG *and glowers at him.*)

DICK: What is your problem?

OG: Shoot—I am sorry, sir—
This is really my first day, honest and I get so nervous—course they said we would and they said when we did to ask the Lord for strength but I asked and I am still so nervous I just louse it up every time.

DICK: You are Og?

OG: Uh...yes, sir.

DICK: Og Oggleby?

OG: Yessir—have we met before, sir?

DICK: Have we, Og?

OG: I don't know sir, but you know my name.

DICK: That's because I'm the devil, Og.

OG: Yes, sir.

DICK: However, you're also wearing a nametag.

OG: Yes, sir.

DICK: And Og—guess what?

OG: What?

DICK: I was kidding about the devil part.

OG: No, sir,
No, I do not believe you were...

DICK: Sin, Og—remember, sin is error.

OG: No, sir, sin is not error—sin is the contravention of the holy word of God which has been set down in the Gospel so that men may know of it and free themselves from it and from temptation and the Devil's Work
For it is surely Devil's Work and nothing else that sends a soul to everlasting torment and damnation through the lure of flesh the snare of pride the goad of envy and the wine of wrath the sting of parsimony and lascivious caress of sloth.

| | |
|---|---|
| For lo the devil's work is manifest in every corner of this land and we are in the last days when the trump shall sound and rend the heavens with its blast And lo the Angel of the Lord appears and with him all the heavenly host in wingéd might, armed in | (GARY *and* M C *reappear in house.*)<br><br>GARY: And hello again sports fans, Gary Cohen welcoming you back to Post Season Baseball—<br>And if you just joined us, we're in an *extended* game delay situation at Shea—so we're talking with a good friend, star of stage and screen and |

righteousness and verily I say
to thee
They shall uproot the wicked and
lay waste to sin
And they shall scourge
damnation from this land in
glory's name....

DICK: Get me OUTTA HERE!!!!

*(Blackout)*

former utility in-and-outfielder
for the old Meerkat League,
The legendary M C Kat...
M C: Yeah, don't forget I also wrote
*Take Me Out to the Ballgame*,
Gary...

# ACT TWO

*(Cowboys sit on the fence, singing "Driving Song.")*

*(DICK and M C in house window, DICK "driving" [i.e. holding a steering wheel])*

COWBOYS:
Acton Afton Aiken Akron
Alamo Allen Alma Alton
Amarillo Ammon Anson Arden
Ardmore Argo Armour Arnold
Ashley Ashton Aspen Atkins
Auburn Austin Ayden Aztec

DICK: I dunno what's going on some kind of goddamn slimeball juju rancid lowlevel scumbag toxic mutant roadkill septic feedbag got no base-on-balls from X prime all the way to Del Ray Beach!

M C: Hey!....

DICK: Anorexic meatball walks the line....

M C: Where am I—in a Wellman play?

Bad axe Bainbridge Baldwin
Bartstow Battle Creek Beaver
Creek Beaver Dam Beech Grove
Bell Glade Bellvue Bellwood
Belton Berlin Berwyn Billerica
Bismarck
Blackburn Blackfoot Bogaloosa
Braintree Brentwood Brookline
Brown Deer Buffalo

DICK: That's "well-made" play, you idiot!

M C: Yeah, well I wish it was—I'd have a bigger part....

*(OG OGGLEBY enters around curtain, his thumb out like a hitchhiker; he moves right, toward house, exiting at a run.)*

OG: Excuse me, sir, I'd like to talk to you about the Loooooooo...

M C: So where am I?

DICK: I dunno.

M C: So where we going?

DICK: Shut up.

M C: You mean we're driving about a hundred and fifty million miles an hour and we don't even know where we're goin'?

DICK: Yeah.

M C: How come?

DICK: Hadda get out of there!

M C: How come?

DICK: Because I said so—now sit down!

M C: Can I drive?

DICK: No.

M C: Can I drive?

DICK: No.

M C: Can I drive?

DICK: You're pushing it....

M C: Can I not drive (ha! ha!—fooled you!)

DICK: How about a long period of silence, okay?

M C: How come?

*(Enter* GARY COHEN*)*

M C: Mind if I turn on the radio?

GARY: And hello again, everybody This is Gary Cohen welcoming you back to another evening of High Concept Baseball where it's always the bottom of the five-hundred and twenty-ninth inning between Despair and the City of Tender Meat with the score tied one oh six to one oh seven.
Alphonzo Beanbag at the plate he takes the cake he passes the plate he takes the gate he doesn't pass go he takes some more cake he's out of control now grimacing wildly he's fuming he's fussing he's well groomed but he's cussing and he-e-e-e-e's out of there—Ball One.

Hey, can I drive when we stop for gas?

Folks I'm on the edge of my seat and I'm not even sitting down,

Didn't hear you say no.

No "no" means yes, okay?

Glad that's settled...
DICK: You're gonna wind up walking if you don't watch out.
M C: Boy you're no fun.

M C: Would you roll down the window?

Would you roll down the window please?

Hey, roll down the window!

I said roll down the window ya big galoot, it's stinky in here!

Thanks for nothing, bozo!

Boy is it boring around here or what?
DICK: Keep your head in!
M C: Who's gonna make me?
DICK: I said keep your head in!
M C: And I said:
Who's gonna make me?
DICK: Keep it in, dammit!
You want to go flying out the window?

What kind of baseball do they play out there?
So that'll bring up Willie the Pimp—
No, let's make that Dan the Old Accordian Man—no, wait—a substitution...
Could be Mack the Knife...
No, I'm sorry, panel—gonna flip over all the cards, because it's actually Quinn the Eskimo—still number two on the charts and he's high and tight—sure wish I could say the same—a light machine gun fire now raking the field sporadically as the band plays on.
Actually, I'm sorry, make that a bank that's playing— I think it's playing either Second Base, or maybe Secondhand Rose— possibly even Secondhand Rosé but still a good year for burgundies, organdies, organ disease and munis.
Woman in curlers just impaled herself on Rusty Staub, she'll need a tetanus shot so as the U S S Ticonderoga sails away behind the batter's box somebody's set my shoe on fire and I'm gonna stop and put it out.
Ball three.
Much better.
Conference on the mound now—line of limos extending down the third base side—I see the shortstop Lizzie Borden in the dugout taking a meat-

M C: Maybe.

DICK: You go flying out the window I'm not stopping to go back for you.

M C: Yeah you will.

DICK: No, you'll be lost! You'll be lost forever.

I couldn't even find you if I tried.

M C: I don't care.

DICK: Just keep your damn head in, damn it!!

M C: Hey, look at me! Hey, I'm dancing! Watch me dance—wanna see? Moonwalk...

Hey, look at this—
This is pretty cool!
Wow!
Oh-oh....

COWBOYS:
Cadillac
Calumet
Camarillo
Camden
Canton
Carson
Charleston
Chelsea
Chicopee
Chippewa
Claremont
Claremore
Clawson
Clayton
Cleveland
Clifton
Clinton
Clovis
Colton
Concord
Cottonwood
Crestwood
Crowley
Crystal

axe to the family—what a pity but we're out of film—

Chili Davis at the plate—

Gooden going with a forkball outside knifeball slicing in—and he gets him with a spoonball! Gooden in the stretch he looks he goes he looks he goes he looks he goes again, sure looks like he's going to go—now he's going to the inside, now he's going to the outside, now he's going to the curve (he can't hang on)—he's going to the hat—no he's going the mound—he's going to the grocery store—I can't believe it—Gooden going going gone to the showers and the fans go wild—

*(As M C flies out window)*

GARY: And folks I have to tell you that right now I have absolutely no idea what's going on on the field...

DICK: Well that makes two of us.

GARY: A little uncertainly of course normal in baseball...

DICK: Any time you're in the broadcast booth...

GARY: Uncertainty principle of course formulated by Werner Heisenberg in 1927 as...

DICK: Oh, come off it, Gary—you're a terrible sports announcer, and you know it!

GARY: Well, I don't actually think I am Big Dick Sorehead (fans getting restless)

DICK: Listen—you're just babbling spew into an open mike and pumping it out across the universe...

GARY: Like to see Big Dick the Sorehead do any better...

DICK: Just watch me.

GARY: Dick the Sorehead of course best remembered for that tragic tragic auto incident when the cute little stuffed animal went...

DICK: Hey—

GARY: Sailing out the window...

DICK: Ixnay on the Uffedstay Imalanay, okay?

GARY: Landing on the highway somewhere out in the middle of nowhere and probably rolling into a ditch...

DICK: Hunh?

GARY: Reports at the time that Dick had been drinking...

DICK: M C????

GARY: And a longstanding animosity between him and the little guy...

DICK: Hey, where is he, you son of a bitch?

GARY: Get your hands off the merchan...

DICK: Where the hell is he!

GARY: I don't know! (Don't hit me!) I don't know...honest... Last thing anybody knew he just went flying out the window...

DICK: You fucking with me?

GARY: *(Trying to cover mike)* Please—watch the *language*...

DICK: If you're fucking with me...

GARY: All right that does it—hit me—hit me! Cause I'll sue your ass so goddam bad *(Covers mike)* godda*mm*it that's fifteen hundred bucks you just cost me!

DICK: Shit!

*(Cowboys screech—GARY slams head on desk.)*

GARY: Now what?

DICK: I gotta go back....

GARY: Back?

DICK: I gotta find him.

GARY: But that's—that's impossible, it's sheer madness!

DICK: Maybe...
But I still gotta try.

GARY: Gee, is it possible that I....

DICK: Hang on little guy—I'm coming...

GARY: ...Misjudged him?

(DICK *steps outside house, crossing to cowboys on fence.*)

DICK: M C????

GARY: Dick...

DICK: M C????

GARY: Hey, wait for me, Dick.

BAD TEX: So, whatchew fellas doin around here anyways...?

DICK: Uhhhhhh...

BAD TEX: Hunh?

DICK: Nothin'.

GARY: Gary Cohen—New York Mets—hey, how are ya, guys?

TEX: This here is private property...

GARY: Totally unaffiliated with the franchise....

DICK: We're lookin' fer somebody.

BAD TEX: Never gonna find 'em.

DICK: I'll find him.

GARY: Strawberry deal—what a disaster....

TEX: Ain't never gonna find 'em without a reward.

GARY: Gooden deal—what a disaster!

DICK: I said I'll find him...

GARY: See, many people don't understand the broadcast end is just a job...

DICK: M C.....

GARY: Jeez, wait up there, will ya...

(DICK *and* GARY *back off S R; beat; cowboys look off in distance.*)

TEX: Looky over yonder.

BAD TEX: Yup.

TEX: You see what I see?

BAD TEX: Well, I don't know—do I?

TEX: Well, whattaya see?

BAD TEX: Injuns....

TEX: Yeah, but next to them injuns.

BAD TEX: Rustlers...

TEX: Yeah, but next to them rustlers...

BAD TEX: What?
You mean the stampede.

TEX: Shoot—not the danged stampede—why any danged fool could see a danged stampede fer fifty miles so what the hell would anybody want to go and call a danged stampede to yer attention for?

BAD TEX: You callin' me a fool?

TEX: Will you just looky over yonder?

BAD TEX: You callin me a fool them's fighting words...

TEX: Just looky over yonder tell me what you see.

BAD TEX: Well...looks like more Injuns

TEX: Yeah, but next to them Injuns.

BAD TEX: Well, looks like them rustlers got the posse after 'em now

TEX: No, dang it—next to them injuns next to them dang rustlers got the posse after 'em...

BAD TEX: Now, dang it—that's that danged stampede—and yer callin me a fool again, ain't you?

TEX: Well, yer talkin' like a fool!

BAD TEX: Tex, them's fighting words!

TEX: Aw, will you just looky over yonder?

BAD TEX: Draw.

TEX: Why don't ya make me.

BAD TEX: I think yer yeller.

TEX: Why don't you prove it.

BAD TEX: You draw.

TEX: You make me.

BAD TEX: I'm callin' yer yeller ya lily-livered, chicken-hearted lowdown son of a sidewindin' sodbusting pussywhipped snake....

*(The cowboys back away from each other,* BAD TEX *disappearing behind house S R as* GARY *and* DICK *enter upstage, around curtain.)*

GARY: Look, I hate to say this, but...

DICK: Then don't...

GARY: But I gotta.

DICK: No, Gary—you don't.

(BAD TEX *enters as* GARY *and* DICK *wander down into crossfire.*)

TEX: Are you prepared to back that up?

GARY: Call it a hunch, call it an intuition,...

DICK: Gary?

GARY: Dick, sometimes you gotta go with what you feel.

DICK: Gary, what did I say...?

GARY: Look, I'm an intuitive kinda guy.

BAD TEX: Are you prepared to draw?

DICK: Gary...

GARY: I just have a bad feeling.

TEX: Are you prepared to make me?

DICK: I don't want to hear about it, Gary.

BAD TEX: Are you prepared to have me call ya yeller?

GARY: Okay, can I just say say one thing?

DICK: No.

GARY: Can I just say I'm having a very very bad bad feeling?

DICK: No.

BAD TEX: Ain't gonna find him, stranger.

DICK: I'll find him.

TEX: Never gonna find him without a reward...

DICK: Look, Gary—
He's my friend okay, maybe not your friend but he's my friend so I have to do this—you don't have to do this—but I have to do this because *I left the window down* and if I don't do something I'll never be able to live with myself because I know he's out there, Gary, and he's tired, and he's hungry, he's scared and I left the window down, so leave me alone!

GARY: You can always get another one, you know?

DICK: Not the same.

GARY: Yeah, but what if he really *is* lost, Dick?

DICK: I'll get another one, now shut up about it!
(*He exits S R, around house.*)

TEX: Okay—now looky over yonder.

BAD TEX: Yup.

GARY: Dumbest thing I ever heard...

TEX: You see what I see?

BAD TEX: Nope.

TEX: Well looky little harder, dang it!

GARY: Actually, the dumbest thing I ever heard was Joe DiMaggio going: "If I'd a been Mister Tea, I'd a had a T V show..."
I mean, great ballplayer but sheesh—what an airhead.

(*Exit* GARY, *following* DICK)

TEX: See it now?

BAD TEX: I don't see nothin' but a cloud of dust.

TEX: Real pokey-like cloud?
Cloud ain't goin' noplace special?
Cloud a feller might say ain't movin' much hardly at all?

BAD TEX: Well he might but he'd be a fool.

TEX: Who's a fool?

BAD TEX: What I'm saying is that there dust cloud is moving so pokey you just cain't see it move is all, but it's movin.

TEX: That's what I said.

BAD TEX: No, you said it warn't moving at all and my position is you jest cain't see it move which ain't the same thing at all.

TEX: Shoot—why don't I just plug you right in the gut.

BAD TEX: Sure like to see you try.

TEX: You keep on a-ridin' me, Tex...

BAD TEX: Don't reckon yer man enough.

TEX: You ready to back that up?

(*Cowboys again back apart as* GARY *and* DICK *enter between them.*)

GARY: It's a big country, Dick—

BAD TEX: Shoot, why don't I just plug you right in the gut my own self?

GARY: Real big country.

TEX: Sure like to see you try.

BAD TEX: You keep on a-ridin' me, Tex.

GARY: One great big huge enormous gigantic wide open mess without a damn thing in it from sea to shining sea, Dick.

DICK: Gary, get lost.

GARY: I am lost, Dick.

TEX: Don't reckon yer man enough.

DICK: Then get lost somewhere else, okay?
Get lost over there.

BAD TEX: You ready to back that up?

GARY: Say, fellas, I wonder if you could help me.
I'm lost.

TEX: Yup.

GARY: Thought you might know where I am?

BAD TEX: Yer lost.

GARY: Any idea where?

BAD TEX: Middle of nowhere.

TEX: Motel's thataway.

GARY: Whichaway? Thisaway?

TEX: Thataway...

GARY: Whichaway? Thisaway?

BAD TEX: Thataway...

GARY: Whichaway? Thisaway?

BAD TEX: Say, I know you—
Yer that broadcast feller with the New York Metropolitans.

GARY: Why yes, yes I am as matter of fact I...

BAD TEX: Rekkunized you the minute you got loused up.

GARY: Oh, why thank you—

BAD TEX: Far as I'm concerned, you could take a blind bear, get him likkered up, set him in a house afire, blow up the house and he'd still do a better job of the play by play than you,
And yer an ugly cuss too, ain't you?

GARY: Fans—they kill me.

TEX: Never gonna find him.

DICK: Just leave me alone!

GARY: Dick...

TEX: Ain't never gonna find him without a reward..

GARY: Let's go, Dick.

(BAD TEX *forces* GARY *off right behind house as* OG *enters.*)

OG: Excuse me, sir, I'd...

DICK: Not now...

OG: Like to take a...

DICK: What the hell is wrong with you, anyway?

OG: Nothing, sir.

DICK: I'll be the judge of that.

OG: 'Cept the fact that I'm a sinner.

DICK: Yeah—I'll bet.

OG: But of course we're all sinners in the eyes of the Lord.

DICK: How come you're everywhere?

OG: Greyhound.

DICK: Yeah, well—why don't you help me for a change.

OG: That is my god-given mission in life, sir.

DICK: See, I'm looking for someone.

OG: Yes, I know.

DICK: *(To* TEX*)* Blabbermouth
Let's say I have this friend, let's say he's a—
Well, let's just call him a friend....

OG: You have a "friend"?

DICK: Now my friend is lost.

OG: But you know in your heart it's not too late for your "friend" to be saved.

DICK: Will you help me, Og?

OG: Oh, sir— *(Kneeling)* Repent ye, for the kingdom of heaven is at hand

DICK: What is this with you?

(DICK *exits right, around house,* OG *following*)

OG: For this is he that was spoken of by the prophet saying....
The voice of one crying in the wilderness...

DICK: Get away—quit following me!

BAD TEX: So just what in tarnation was that dustball thing, Tex?

TEX: Tex—that there's The Lonesome Poke.
Just a-ridin on his faithful palomino, Slow.

(*Cowboys exit upstage as* MONICA *enters from back of audience.*)

MONICA: Wouldn't it be nice if the Creator installed a little switch in us so that when we didn't have any control over a situation we could simply flip it and our worrying would cease? You know—your daughter marries this guy who's no good—you just flip the switch:
You say, "I don't like this, but nothing I can do, so I'll just be philosophical and not worry!!!"

(BOB HOWARD *enters around upstage corner of house and sulks.*)

MONICA: Now personally, I've flown so much—that is—
I'm so desensitized,
That I feel the same on a plane as in my own living room.

BOB: You got another man, babe...

MONICA: So, if it's a bad flight,
I just go to sleep.

BOB: Cause I've seen you.

MONICA: Because there's nothing I can do....

BOB: And if I had any pride at all I'd go, but I don't....

MONICA: If I'm going to crash, I'm going to crash.

BOB: And I don't care.

MONICA: And obviously, if that happens,
I'd rather be asleep.

BOB: Tryin' hard babe, but if I can't have you I don't want to try....

MONICA: Now a couple years ago, I'm on a flight with a real "white knuckles" type.
And of course, the weather's so bad, we're forced down on some Air Force base in Indiana.
I'm trying to sleep—but this guy—let's call him he/she—
He/she's pushing the call button, telling the flight attendant to tell the pilot certain things,
Trying to control the plane by controlling the pilot by controlling the flight attendant.

BOB: I tried to drink you off my mind

MONICA: He/she's talking to God

BOB: I sat up in the bed and cried....

MONICA: Trying to control the weather by controlling God.
He/she's doing everything in the world to try to control a situation over which there was absolutely no control.

BOB: And it cuts me babe, it cuts me hard,
I'm just all busted up and bleeding on the inside.

MONICA: Now, there's a newspaper on the seat between us,

BOB: I'm goin down...

MONICA: And the headline's all about this lake in Africa that had poison gas at the bottom and the pressure on the gas just built up to the point where it bubbled up and hundreds and thousands of cows and people were killed.

BOB: I'm just so gone it's really pitiful—I'm sick 'n low and here I come right back for more

MONICA: And he/she's worried about this lake near his home.

BOB: Baby, baby—say you love me,

MONICA: What if there's poison gas in the lake?

BOB: I don't care if it's a lie.

MONICA: What if the gas comes up and kills people?

BOB: Cure me, baby—can't you cure me?

MONICA: A classic example of unless worry in a situation where there's no control.
Obviously if you lived by a lake full of poison gas
What could you do except be philosophical...

(MONICA *exits through audience, leaving* BOB *at the edge of the stage; he turns and exits up right, behind house; fade to black.*)

M C: *(Off)* Hey?
Where am I?
(*Lights up; actress who plays* M C *is upstage holding the doll.*)
Hey, where am I?
Hey, ya big galoot....

DICK: *(Off)* M C??

M C: Yeah, here I am... here I am....

GARY: *(Off)* M C????

M C: Yeah—You found me! Over here! Over here! Come back here!

DICK: *(Off)* M C???

M C: No, back here... Hey, come back, guys..

GARY: *(Off)* Dick, I know we already looked here.

DICK: *(Off)* Yeah, guess you're right.

M C: No, I'm here! You can find me! Help! Help! Save me!
Saaaaaaaaaave Me-e-e-e-e-e-e (Wow, what an echo)
Help, -elp-elp-elp...
Get me out-ut-ut-ut of-f-f-f- here-ere-ere-ere-ere!
(Oh, boy, I am getting a real bad feeling about this...)
*(M C crosses downstage along fence.)*
Calling all cars, calling all cars, this is M C Kat, over...Do you read me? Over...
Oh, this is really terrible—whose idea was this, I wanna complain!
Free Money! Come and get yer free money!
Oh, boy, and I didn't even pack a sleeping bag or anything—I CAN'T BELIEVE THIS HAPPENING TO ME!!
Anybody out here?
Oh, what am I gonna do?

*(cowboys enter upstage, running in slow motion.)*

| | |
|---|---|
| *(M C starts to cry)*<br>M C: I'm not scared.<br>I just wanna go home | TEX & BAD TEX: W-o-o-o-o-o-o-o-oo—<br>W-o-o-o-o-o-o-o-o... |
| Yeah I know, that's what I'm afraid of.... | You ain't gonna like it here,<br>little fella. |
| Wait a minute....<br>Who said that? | You ain't gonna like it here<br>at all... |

*(Cowboys sing.)*

| | |
|---|---|
| Oh, boy—you ever get the feelin' yer in trouble?<br>Lemme tell ya, it's a lousy feelin'...<br>Oh-oh...<br>Better get outta here.<br>Help!<br>Lemmmmme outta here<br>Gemme outta here<br>Heeeeeeeeellllllp! | TEX & BAD TEX: Here we come,<br>On the run<br>Here we come,<br>On the run<br>Hey, we're out here<br>and we're coming at you...<br>We're out here<br>and we're gonna getcha! |

*(Blackout)*

# ACT THREE

*(CITIZEN is in the house, reading a newspaper; DICK enters; he pays no attention until DICK coughs.)*

CITIZEN: Yeah?

DICK: I'd like a room.

CITIZEN: No pets.

DICK: I don't have any pets.

CITIZEN: You just lost one, didn't you?

DICK: No, I didn't just lose him, he fell out—it was an accident, okay?

CITIZEN: Pet gopher?

DICK: What makes you so well-informed all of a sudden?

CITIZEN: Small town gossip.

DICK: Yeah, well for your information I didn't lose a pet gopher—
He's not a pet, he fell, and he's a Meerkat.

CITIZEN: What the hell you go foolin' with gophers for? Hunh?
What the hell kind of fool pet is that?
Gopher ain't no pet—
Hey, I'm talking to you.
You damn city folk think you're so smart, well, you listen mister Smarty—you get a little kid round that gopher and that kid gets bit or chewed or scratched or even has a little cut on his finger when he handles him, you know what?
That kid could have to git the rabies treatment—
You ever think of that? I doubt it—
But if yer gopher has the rabies and that kid don't get the treatment he'll be dead by Sunday and you know how bad the rabies is—my god, you see a squirrel, coon or possum got the rabies you just put him down, you put him down right there, but I don't s'poze city folk know about that, now do they?
Hell, do you know even know what the rabies treatment is?

DICK: Yeah, it's fourteen shots in the belly.

CITIZEN: It's fourteen agonizing shots in the belly every day, one a day, in the belly, fourteen days, in a row, pore little kid howlin' his head off, but you city folk never think of that, do you?

DICK: Look, he doesn't bite, see.

CITIZEN: Oh, you can say that—sure, you know that, don't you?

DICK: No—he doesn't bite, okay—you know why?
Cause he got his mouth sewed shut! Does that satisfy you?

CITIZEN: Sewed shut? God, you city folk is heartless.

DICK: Whattaya have to do to get a drink around here?

CITIZEN: Wait here...

(GARY *appears in upstage house window as* CITIZEN *exits.*)

GARY: Oh and two the count and the pitch to Tudor low and outside for a ball
So it's one and two.

DICK: Hey, is there anything else on?

GARY: Tudor oh for two—popped out to short and a line drive deep to center in the fifth....

DICK: Mind if I change the channel?

(GARY *hands* DICK *a remote control device.*)

GARY: Be my guest—so it's oh and two the count and....
Oh and two the count and the pitch to Barnswell low...
...and two the count and the pitch to Vasquez low...
...and two the count and the pitch to...
Center in the fifth...
*Aqui, señoras y señores...*
Oh and two the count and the pitch to Tudor low and outside for a ball...
So it's one and two...

(CITIZEN *enters D R in front of house, crossing into front window.*)

CITIZEN: What'll it be?

DICK: Whatya got?

CITIZEN: On tap—Smood County.

DICK: Smood County?

CITIZEN: Local beer.

GARY: Oh and two the count and the pitch is low...

DICK: What's in bottles?

CITIZEN: Smood Light, Heineken.

GARY: So it's one and two...

DICK: That's it?

CITIZEN: Ran out of Smood.

DICK: I'll have a margarita.

CITIZEN: Straight up, rocks or slush?

DICK: Straight up.

CITIZEN: With salt, no salt?

DICK: No salt.

CITIZEN: Blue?

DICK: Regular.

CITIZEN: Got a choice of your blue marlin, your mermaid or your dolphin swizzle?

DICK: No umbrellas?

CITIZEN: Margarita—that's with the tequila, right?

GARY: Got that herky-jerky motion kinda reminds you of Tiant...

DICK: You mind a personal question?

CITIZEN: You mind a poke in the nose?

DICK: You related to the guy runs the motel?

CITIZEN: Nope.

GARY: Jams him inside...

CITIZEN: Just a small town, you know—inbreeding, I guess....

DICK: Beats ice-fishing.

CITIZEN: You here for the turkey-shoot?

DICK: No, I'm looking for a friend *(Shows picture in wallet)*—
Seen him around?

CITIZEN: Meerkat, hunh?
Yeah—we had one in here once,
Till he got mixed up with a prairie dog and fell out the window.

DICK: Yeah, well they can't hold their booze, it's a problem.

(CITIZEN *exits D S R; S L, M C on downstage fencepost.*)

M C: Days and nights across the burning sand...
I cry for water... "Water"... but there is no water...
This is it—I can't go on... and yet I must go on.
Ohhhhh—this is hell—this is agony...

My feet are all scuffed up—this is an outrage—I want to complain—
I shouldn't have to walk—I'm the star!
Taxi! Taxi!—Oh, no—it's stopping.
I must be hallu-u-u-u-u-u-u-u-cinating.....
Yes—palm trees—Wayne Newton...
I'm going insaaaaannnnnneee! Ah-ha-ha-ha-haaaaaaa!
"In his desert scenes,
M C Kat delivers a performance of heartbreaking verisimilitude"
Mel Gussow, *New York Times*....

(CITIZEN, *in drag, enters house and sits S L in window.*)

CITIZEN: I'll have a double Tanqueray martini up very dry with a twist and I'd like to see a menu, please.

GARY: I'm sorry ma'am, I'm just the televison,

DICK: Bartender just stepped away....

GARY: So it's one and two...

DICK: You'll know him—kinda looks like you.

GARY: Tudor oh for two—popped out to short and a line drive deep to center in the fifth...

CITIZEN: Hell, everybody looks like everybody else in these dinky towns.

DICK: Inbreeding.

CITIZEN: Actually, it's the Land's End Catalog.

GARY: Had a little control problem earlier but Stottlemeyer seems to have settled him right down...

CITIZEN: I'm Mary, with Merrill, in futures.

DICK: I'm Dick, and I'm not.

CITIZEN: That's cute, Dick—

DICK: Any future in futures?

CITIZEN: Well I don't think the economic downswing is structural if that's what you mean.

DICK: So I take it you're not in town for the turkey shoot?

CITIZEN: Dick, I find you attractive so let's cut to the chase.
I'm on a tight schedule, but if I can switch my 8:05 to Raleigh to the 9:23, I think we'll have enough time for sex.

DICK: Hunh?

CITIZEN: Sex, Dick—we're going to have sex:
I'm going to enjoy it, you might want to do the same.

DICK: Can I get back to you on that one, Mare?

CITIZEN: No, Dick—now. I'm going to need three to four minutes to call in to my office,
Why don't you rustle up something from room service?

DICK: Mary, something tells me they don't have a whole heck of a lot of room service here at the Wanderlust Motel.

CITIZEN: With Merrill, Dick,
There is always room service and we never take no for an answer.
*(She pulls a telephone receiver out of her bag.)*
Suzie, darling, hi, it's Kay, glad I caught you.
Listen, honey, get me on the 9:26 to Raleigh, would you? Thanks, and I'll need another car on that—now, call Stan, tell him I'm running late but there's Stouffers—and Suzie, I'm in 436 at something called the Wanderlust Motel—could you track down room service and have them send a bottle of Remy and a couple of Trojans?
Yeah...
Any faxes? Super. Check the voice mail? Yeah. Got it, got it, got it, (this'll just take a minute) got it, shit when did that happen?
Yeah, scratch the 9:26, I'll take the 6:16, cancel the room service, tell Ralph to run the numbers and I want Vince and Roger in my office in two hours!
Sorry, Dave—gotta run—some damn idiot just blew up France and now I'm gonna have to pull an all nighter! *(She exits.)*

GARY: Still oh and two the count and you know, Dick Sorehead,
It's really a sad crazy lonely mixed up kind a world we live in.
A world of frightened little people and their pathetic tinsel dreams.

DICK: Here's looking at you, Gary.

GARY: We'll always have Paris, Dick.

DICK: Apparently not.

*(The curtain rises:* POKE *centerstage on a sawhorse, singing.)*

POKE: So here I come just ridin' slow
Done rode from Maine to Mexico
But where I'm bound don't rightly know
'Cause I ain't got no place to go

*(Spoken)* Dear Folks—
Been another long lonesome hot and dusty day in the saddle without much to show for it.
Signed, the Poke.
P S: Still lonesome.
*(Singing)* So here I come....

*(Enter* TEX *and* BAD TEX; *they come up to the* POKE.)

POKE: And a great big western-style howdy to you fellas and I shore would love to stop 'n set a spell but I'm a coming through so boys you best stand clear get out the way yaaaaaaa-hooooooo, ride 'em, cowboy.

TEX: Now just hold yer horses, stranger—

POKE: Whoa, Slow....

TEX: Say, ain't you the hombre known east of the Rockies 'n' west of the Pecos 'n' north of the border 'n' south of the Rio Grande as The Lonesome Poke?

POKE: Well...

BAD TEX: Or ain't you?

POKE: Well...

BAD TEX: Well, what?

POKE: Guess so.

TEX: Why—ain't you sure about that?

POKE: Well...

BAD TEX: Well, what?

POKE: Guess so.

TEX: Come on, partner, hurry it up there, hurry it up.

POKE: Caint.

TEX: How come?

POKE: Well...

BAD TEX: What, dang it?

POKE: Kinda pokey, I guess.

BAD TEX: I'll say.

POKE: See, I come from well I come from no place, I guess, or well no place special I guess and I'm headed well I'm headed...

TEX: Worse'n watchin' grass grow after ya mowed it.

POKE: Heck I guess I'm headed...

BAD TEX: Worse'n watchin' paint dry after it's dry already.

POKE: Come to think of it I just don't know where I'm headed fellas but I'm ridin' slow and just takin my time.
Slow's my horse, of course.

BAD TEX: Ain't much of a horse.

POKE: Well, she's trusty.

TEX: Ain't even much of a sawhorse, for that matter....

POKE: Boys, ain't nothin' the matter with Slow except she's—well she's, now she's just, just a little bit...

BAD TEX: Poke, tell ya what—think it's time I showed ya how to speed her up some...

POKE: Well...

BAD TEX: Haw! *(Kicks the sawhorse)*
Giddyup there, horsey...

POKE: Now, fellers...

TEX: Believe she's runnin' just a little bit faster there, Tex.

POKE: Hold it, fellers...

BAD TEX: Do believe she is, but watch me now!
Haw! *(Kicks the sawhorse)*
Shoot she's a ball of fire, if ya know how to treat her!

TEX: My turn....

POKE: Please, fellas...

BAD TEX: Try and kick her like this, Tex... *(Kicks)*

TEX: You mean, like this? *(Kicks)*

BAD TEX: Like this! *(Kicks)*

POKE: Don't kick my horse, boys...

TEX: Wait—now, show me again...

POKE: Oh, fellas...

BAD TEX: Gotta kick 'er like so...

TEX: Like so?

BAD TEX: ...Like so.

TEX: ...Like so?

BAD TEX: ...Like so.

TEX: ...Like so?

POKE: Now cut that out!!!

TEX & BAD TEX: What?

POKE: Well, I asked you proper but you wouldn't listen.

BAD TEX: Poke—you wanna fight about it?

POKE: Well...

BAD TEX: Well, what?

POKE: No, but...

TEX: Chicken....

POKE: Will if I have to.

BAD TEX: Well, I guess you heard him, Tex.

TEX: I heard him call you down, Tex.

POKE: I reckon I called you down, Tex, yup I reckon I did.

BAD TEX: Reckon one of us gots to die now, Poke. Sure hope it ain't you.

TEX: Sure hope it ain't.

POKE: Thanks...

BAD TEX: Cause it sure ain't gonna be me!
Haw! Haw! Haw! Haw!

TEX: Say, Poke—ya fast?

POKE: S-sorta fast.

BAD TEX: You ready?

POKE: Well...

BAD TEX: Call it, Tex!

TEX: Draw!

BAD TEX: Go fer your guns!

POKE: I'm... *(He doesn't appear to move.)* ...a-drawin....

TEX: Draw, Poke, draw!

POKE: I'm a-drawin, boys—I'm a-makin my move!...

TEX: Come on—Draw down, Poke!

POKE: Heck, I am—why ain't *you* a-drawin, Tex?

BAD TEX: Is he movin', Tex, cause I cain't tell?

POKE: I'm movin, boys, I'm movin!

TEX: Cain't tell if he ain't movin' or just ain't appeared to move.

POKE: No, it's comin, boys—and it's a glorious move....

BAD TEX: Tell you what, Poke—
You get a head start, and I'll come back 'n kill ya later...

POKE: But I got a good move, Tex—honest!

BAD TEX: Buy you a drink?

TEX: Sounds good to me.

POKE: Aw, come back fellas,
I'm drawin as fast as I can....

*(Curtain falls as cowboys exit S R; in house, CITIZEN in U S L corner.)*

GARY: "Sheesh, this upset stomach's really getting to me..."

CITIZEN: You got big hands.

GARY: That ever happen to you?

DICK: Yeah, I guess.

GARY: Because sometimes out at the ballpark the action won't give you a chance to eat right.

CITIZEN: You like to squeeze things?

GARY: So when too many peanuts and crackerjacks cross your plate,
Reach for major league relief.

CITIZEN: I do.

GARY: Reach for Digestin.

CITIZEN: But I don't have big hands.
So what are you really here for, anyway?

DICK: Looking for a meerkat.

CITIZEN: I mean really.

DICK: I'm serious.

CITIZEN: I'm not gonna tell anybody.

DICK: I'm telling you the truth.

CITIZEN: D S A, or you with the Bureau?

DICK: It's just what I told you.

CITIZEN: So you can't talk about it, right?

DICK: There's nothing to talk about.

CITIZEN: It's the saucers, isn't it?

DICK: Really just looking for a meerkat.

CITIZEN: Okay, now listen,
I can't swear to it, but they did have a female in there too, and even though she was covered up pretty good I have since come across a number of photos showing tattoos and other distinguishing marks which have convinced me that it was Cher.

DICK: Thanks—I'll keep that in mind.

CITIZEN: My pleasure.

DICK: Now let me ask you:
Have you ever seen anything that looked like this? *(Shows wallet)*

CITIZEN: Jesus Christ—it ain't even human, is it?

DICK: Just let me know if you see it—

CITIZEN: Mister, I don't know who you are, and I never even seen you, okay?
But you will have my one hundred percent cooperation on this.
And I just want to let you and anyone else who might be interested know—
There was many of us here believed Mister Hoover would have been the
    best damn president this country ever had.

DICK: Thank you. *(They shake hands.)*

CITIZEN: Squeeze it
Squeeze on it good.
Harder, damn it!
There—that's good....

*(CITIZEN exits; curtain rises: POKE and cowboys as before.)*

TEX: Ain't it just the most miserable move you ever did see?

POKE: Called you down, Tex, yup—now one of us got to die!

BAD TEX: Shoot he ain't moved at all.

POKE: No, here it come, now...

TEX: Well, a little...

BAD TEX: No he ain't.

POKE: Boys, I'm makin my move now....

TEX: Well, a little.

BAD TEX: No, he ain't...

POKE: Here it come, now, boys and it's gonna be a beauty....

BAD TEX: And I say he ain't moved at all....

TEX: And I'm callin' you a liar.

POKE: Stand over there, Tex...

BAD TEX: Hell, them's fighting words.

POKE: Would you stand over there so I can shoot ya, Tex?

TEX: *(Drawing a line in the dirt)* Step over this...

POKE: Now, wait a minute, boys.

BAD TEX: I dare you to make me.

POKE: Hey, now come back, Tex...

TEX: An' I dare you to dare me!

POKE: Dang it, Tex—you just come back here!
I was fightin' you first and I was fightin' you fair and I was makin' my move and it's a mighty fine move so you come on back here and fight!
Aw, shoot!

*(Cowboys back off behind curtain; POKE sits on sawhorse, sulks.)*

POKE: Won't nobody never fight with me nowhow er nothing—
Swear I never get no fun, nope—never did, never will—
And there ain't no justice in the world.
But I aim ta git me a quick draw holster from the Sears 'n Roebuck, and well sir, then you watch me—
I won't fight with nobody never mind how nice they ask.

*(M C appears around S L edge of curtain.)*

M C: Saved—I'm going to live!!! Hooray for meeeeeee!

POKE: Aw shut up ya danged fool what cause you got to be happy for?

M C: (Ah, civilization—yes, it all comes back to me now...)
So what's your problem, jerkface?

POKE: Yer my problem, ya noisy little rodent.
Cain't you see I'm downhearted and my head is hung low?
Now shut up and beat it!

M C: Ya wanna make me, galoot-brain?

POKE: Listen ya pesky varmint—
If I had my way I'd stomp yer pointy head, skin yer mangy little hide and roast yer scrawny carcass on an open spit, but unfortunately—
I'm fightin' somebody else right now,
So you'll just have to wait!

M C: Yeah—excuses, excuses—so how 'bout a ride, hunh?
Get me out of here, you know—rescue me?

POKE: Don't know, don't care, don't give a dang.

M C: Yeah, what a guy, what a guy, thanks a million.
So where you headed, partner?

POKE: Don't know, don't care, don't give a dang.

M C: Yeah, real snappy conversationalist, too—aren't you?
So—you mind if I drive, hunh?
Take a spell at the wheel?
Driving's one of my special skills, you know.

POKE: Don't know, don't care, don't...

M C: Yeah—get outta my way—
Oh, boy—watch me drive real fast.
Here we go now—gittyap there, horsey!
Yahoo—ride'em cowboy!
Wait a minute—what's the deal here—
Is this thing broken broken?

POKE: Now you just shut up about my horse:
'Cause she's slow and she's stupid and old and ornery and ugly and splintery and all beat to heck but she's mine and I love her so don't you go kickin' her, neither...

M C: You ever run into a guy named Dick Sorehead?

POKE: Nope.

M C: Remind me, I'll introduce you...

*(Curtain falls;* CITIZEN *and* DICK *in house.)*

GARY: May 23 Mets Homeless Person Day—
All fans tweenty-five years and older to receive a Homeless Person courtesy of the New York City Housing Authority....

CITIZEN: Sell ya a milker.

DICK: Beg pardon...

CITIZEN: Milkin' machine,
Sell it to ya cheap—I'm just a little be-hind on payments if you know what I mean.

DICK: I'm from New York....

GARY: June Fifth, Mets Scofflaw Day...

CITIZEN: Never know when it might come in handy

GARY: All fans to receive an outstanding parking violation...

CITIZEN: Pretty color, too—shiny—

DICK: Thanks, but...

CITIZEN: Throw in the sow.
Your sow's milk's closest thing to mother's milk there is, plus you got your sow cheese, cottage cheese, and yoghurt—tangy...

DICK: I'm in a walk-up.

CITIZEN: Where abouts?

DICK: Tribeca.

CITIZEN: You know Al Bridge? He's in Tribeca.

DICK: No, I don't know Al Bridge.

GARY: June 15th the Knights of Columbus sponsoring Racial Tension Day—
All fans to receive a genuine Louisville Slugger...

CITIZEN: Sheepshears—sell 'em to you cheap!
Think about it 'fore you say no: there's a recession on.

GARY: And of course, Cardinal O'Connor hosting Wrath of God Day June 29th...
All fans not married in the eyes of the church to receive a sexually transmitted disease...

CITIZEN: Loan me some money?

DICK: How much?

CITIZEN: Forty-seven hundred dollars and eighty-nine cents.

DICK: Are you crazy?

CITIZEN: No sir—broke, desperate hungry, scared and suicidal, that's all.

(*Enter* OG.)

OG: Sir...

DICK: Now what!

OG: I'd like to talk to you about, you know,
Your "friend" who's lost?

DICK: Yeah, but before you start Og, one simple question—have you found him?

OG: Have I found Him?

DICK: Simple English question, Og—

OG: Yes, sir, I have found Him

DICK: Really?

OG: Yessir—and I'd like you to find Him too.

DICK: Great—where is he?

OG: In your heart, sir.

DICK: Don't mess with me, Og.

OG: I am not, sir—I am trying with all my heart and soul to help you find Him too—but you rebuff me.

CITIZEN: Aw fer chrissake Ogden don't be a crybaby.

OG: Didn't he rebuff me.

DICK: Og, if you know where he is, please just tell me.

OG: Well, He's in Heaven, like you didn't know it.

DICK: You mean he's dead.

OG: Yes, sir.

DICK: Yeah, I guess I was afraid of that.
Okay, just take me to the body.

OG: Body, sir? What body sir?

DICK: Thought you said he was dead.

OG: Yes, sir.

DICK: Then where's the body?

OG: Well I don't know sir—
That was an awful long time ago.

DICK: Have you seen him or not, Og?

OG: But that's not as easy a question as you make it sound.

DICK: Lemme show you a picture, Og.
You ever seen anything that looks like this?

OG: Is that a stuffed animal, sir?

CITIZEN: Can I see that?
*(He takes the wallet, drinks up and exits.)*

DICK: Yeah, he is a stuffed animal but if I ever hear you call him that again I'll bust you one, ok?

OG: Yes, sir—but I don't care what you do to me,
That is not our Lord and Saviour Jesus Christ, sir.

DICK: Who ever said that it was?

OG: Well, I'm naming no names but they mocked Jesus too.

DICK: What the hell is wrong with this guy—
Hey—where'd he go?
Where's my wallet?
Hey—he took my wallet.

*(Enter CITIZEN in front of house as before; GARY in window.)*

CITIZEN: Nother round?
DICK: I just got robbed!
CITIZEN: Un-hunh.

DICK: What do you mean—
"Unhunh?"

GARY: Howdy wranglers
Texas Gary Cohen talkin' to
ya from the House O'Cash
sayin if you need cash fer
any reason just mosey on
down ta ma good buddies
at the House O Cash
They'll fix ya right up and
you cannot be refused for

CITIZEN: Heard it all before...

It comes to three-fifty...
DICK: But I was robbed...
Wasn't I robbed?
You were here, you saw it!
OG: Didn't see nothin'
DICK: Oh—come on—you were
   here, you saw the man
   take my wallet...
OG: The Bible teaches: Thou
   Shalt not Bear False
   Witness
CITIZEN: And it's three fifty.

DICK: Can you loan it to me?

OG: Beg your pardon?
DICK: Can you loan me some
   goddamn money please
   and shut up about it—
What the hell kind of damn
   Christian are you,
      anyway?
OG: The Bible teaches turn the
   other cheek.
That is the only reason I am
   loaning you money and it
   in no way implies that I
   condone intoxicating
   spirits.
DICK: Gimme a ten, okay?
OG: Three fifty and a thirty five
   cent tip comes to
Three eight five round it off
Four dollars....

any reason.
Say ya need a little long
   green fer the home-
   improvement school-
   need health-need auto
   whatnot we don't care go
   *take* that luxury vacation
   folks we just don't give a
   damn just swing on by
   and bring the truck
   cause we got too much
   cash it's sittin around we
   gotta git rid of it.

Folks, remember, it don't
   matter what yer situation
   is if you are still alive you
   have some assets and
   nobody but a danged
   fool sets on his assets
   when he could be setting
   on some cold hard cash
   so come on down we
   give you cash for your
   assets cold hard cash on
   the barrel-head just as
   simple as that and you
   remember folks we got
   the easy terms we got
   the long repayment plan
   you cannot be refused
   for any reason.
So folks, when you need
   dough ray me don't go fa
   just come on down to the
   House O' Cash where the
   secret ingredient is....

(OG *pays the* CITIZEN, *then exits, followed by* CITIZEN.)

GARY: "Skcabneerg"—that's "Greenbacks" spelled sideways—
'Cause folks we got that money to burn *(Lights a bill)*
And we got that service with a smile because
We're jes' plain loco, folks!!!
So long!

(*Enter* MONICA *up center,* BOB HOWARD *around house*)

MONICA: The Type A Behavior Person or T A B P—
Hard-driving, ambitious, time-urgent, multiphasic, impatient, chronically worked up and one very very angry human being—

BOB: Sheesh—this upset stomach's really getting to me....

MONICA: Bank lines, restaurant lines, post office lines—any kind of line'll drive 'em crazy.

BOB: I feel...terrible, this gas pain is (Whoa!)—
Really making me nauseous—

MONICA: You watch a T A B P in the supermarket it'll bring tears to your eyes.

BOB: Musta been something I ate....

MONICA: First they get in the short line, turns out to be the slow line, checker is a Type B, sacker is Type B, Type B woman in front has a giant stack of coupons, has to write a check, then decides to balance her checkbook....

BOB: Sure wish I could just lie down for a second...

MONICA: I had a T A B P tell me once, "Doctor, when I die, I pray to God there's an express line into heaven."

BOB: Hoo boy—I don't *know*—what the hell did I eat...?

MONICA: "Eight sins or less, you go right through."

BOB: Christ—I'm all clammy.

MONICA: Because if anything goes wrong, if a T A B P misses a turn driving, or forgets something and has to go back, they become incredibly worked up.
And when you get worked up,

BOB: Man, this isn't going away.....

MONICA: Your body secretes adrenalin.

BOB: Oh, that was bad, that was bad, that was bad—it's really bad.

MONICA: Now adrenalin was created for emergencies.

BOB: God—it's bad.

MONICA: You read accounts of accidents where women lift cars off pinned-down victims. How could they could do it?

BOB: Oh, god—don't let it be a heart attack.

MONICA: Adrenalin.
Problem is adrenalin has an incredibly toxic effect on

BOB: Oh, God, don't wanna have a heart attack.

your coronary arteries. It works fine for occasional emergencies, but if you secrete too often, it's like drain cleaner, it just eats a hole in the pipe
And you see people start spilling adrenalin the minute their feet hit that floor in the morning, they just keep on spilling that stuff all day just talking on the phone or supervising their secretary or even opening the mail, just spilling adrenaline, burning a hole in their arteries and a hole in the artery makes the fat snag and a molecule of fat that stays there longer than three days becomes permanently bonded so the blockage enlarges and the build-up produces a coronary occlusion and bingo—
There you go...

BOB: Oh man—I feel so bad I feel so bad.

*(By now BOB has collapsed against the fence and is struggling to get off.)*

BOB: Oh God please help me God please help me God.
Help me Jesus help me
Jesus please don't let me die

Oh help me God please help me God please help me help me help me help me

*(Somehow BOB manages to make it off behind curtain.)*

(MONICA *exits D S R.*)

(*Curtain opens, revealing* POKE *and* M C *riding slow and singing.*)

POKE: So here I come little dogie ridin' slow

    M C: Little Dogie

And I'm headed for that roundup in the sky

    Little Dogie

Been from Santa Catalina to the Badlands of
Dakota
But I'll never git back home until I die

I'm headed home

    Ya-hoo!

I long to get there

                    Yippie yi yo

And I'll be there with ya
   darlin by and by
                    Ride 'em cowboy!

No more to roam
This lonesome trail of
   sorrows
Cause you never get to
Heaven till you die

M C: Wow, that's sad.

POKE: Yup.

M C: I mean, it's still pretty cool, you know, but it's sad.
Uh, anyway, Uh, I know a song but it's not really sad.
It's more traditional and bloody—it's a hornpipe, acutally—I wrote it
   myself, it's pretty cool....
Yay for MEEEEEEE!
So you want me to sing it for you? Hunh? Hunh?
Pleeeeeeeeeease—I won't screw it up, I'll do a good job. I promise—okay?
Okay, here goes!
Okay, (xeh-xeh) here we go!
Okay, (ahem) here we go now!
Here we go!
Ohhhhhhh... (Uh, was that A sharp minor or just a goodlooking teenager?
Ah, never mind!)

*(Sings)* Oh, there once was a river that ran to the sea
And it goes by the name of the Rose of Tralee
Ah but me and my true love shall nevermare be free
Till the fat guy in front of us gets up to pee

Singing hey diddle-diddle hey diddle-diddle hey diddle-diddle diddle
   quack-quack-quack (wait a minute, how'd the ducks in here?)
Hey diddle-diddle ooompah-pah-pah
Yodel-odel-odel-odel-ay-hee-hoo (regular alpine wonderland here)

And they sang to the stars with their backs to the wall
And they laughed and they cried and they started to fall
And the good ones were fat but the fat ones were small
So just who in the hell is this Bobby Magee

Singing hey-diddle-diddle hey-diddle-diddle hey-diddle-diddle
quack-quack-quack!
Hey diddle-diddle ay-hee-hoo
*(Bang!)*

*(Cowboys have entered and stand by POKE.)*

POKE: Howdy, fellas...

M C: Sorry about that—duck season came up kinda sudden...

TEX: Poke, you know what time it is?

POKE: Well, lemme see now, boys, must be kinda early, yup, make that exactly four fifteen in the morning, wait a minute, got a little later now, comin up on four sixteen, yup, just about....

BAD TEX: Poke you know us, me an Tex...

POKE: Yup.

TEX: And you know we's patient men that don't rile easy....

POKE: Nope—I mean, yup.

BAD TEX: But there is one thing riles us—
Riles us good...

TEX: Riles us real good...

BAD TEX: Riles us real real good:
And that's some jackass singin when we're sleepin!

M C: Aw shut up, ya big galoot.

BAD TEX: Poke, yer pet just called me a big galoot.

M C: Wait a minute! I'm not a pet!

BAD TEX: And them's fightin' words...

M C: I'm nobody's pet—you wanna fight about it!

TEX: Draw down, Poke!

POKE: Heck, I'm still a drawin' from the last time, Tex!

M C: POW!

BAD TEX: I gotcha, Poke!

POKE: Yup, looks like ya got me, Tex.

M C: POW! POW! POW!

TEX: Got ya too, Poke!

BAD TEX: Yeah, but I got ya first.

TEX: Yeah, but I got ya worse.

POKE: Yeah, looks bad, boys.

TEX: Looks like he gotcha bad but I gotcha real real bad.

POKE: It's the gutshot, Tex and Tex.

BAD TEX: Ooooooooh, that's bad.

POKE: Real bad.

TEX: Real real real bad.

TEX: Oooooooooooooooooh, that's real real bad.

BAD TEX: Real bad

TEX: Real real real bad.

TEX: So I reckon yer pretty much fixin' to die, Poke.

POKE: Well...

BAD TEX: Well, what?

POKE: Well, I'm dying, boys, I'm dying real good, but I'm just well, shoot, I'm jest takin my time is all you know, doin' it slow and pokey-like which after all is my fashion and I don't mean to keep you boys but I know from experience won't do no good to rush me and it might take oh about forty more years and meanwhile boys remember that move? Well I'm just about ready to make that move and here she come and boys she's a one in a million!

TEX & BAD TEX: Awwwwwwwww, ya got us both ya got us bad.
It was a gut shot Poke.

POKE: Yup, it's bad!

TEX: Feel like I'm fixin to die, Tex.

BAD TEX: Tex, I'm fixin to die myself.

TEX & BAD TEX: Poke, turn my face to the wall, Poke!

TEX: Me first.

BAD TEX: No, me—turn me first, Poke.

TEX: Me, me, me.

POKE: Boys—

TEX: But he shot me first.

BAD TEX: But he shot me worse.

POKE: Now don't be fighting, boys...

M C: Oh, nooooooooooo!

TEX & BAD TEX: What wuz that!

M C: Oh, Tex and Tex you got me everywhere I'm perforated and it's horrible terrible godawful badass bad boys and it's getting worse—wow, that smarts!

BAD TEX: What the hell is he doin in our scene?

M C: Boys, don't leave me, boys, don't leave me cause I'm tired of living
   and skeered of dying and I'm headed 'cross the wide Missouri.
And now: the dying words of M C Kat, by M C Kat as he was dying...
Of which Michael Feingold writes in the *Village Voice*:
"A brilliant interpretation of my translation of Sardou"...

TEX: Little glory hog is what I'd say.

M C: Friends, roadhands, country people of all genders,
Lend me a buck and a half.

BAD TEX: Wait a minute
He ain't hurt so bad....

M C: I come to Barre Vermont, but not in turd!

TEX: Shoot...he ain't hurt at all as near as I can tell....

M C: *(Shut up)* The good that men do is evil—
So let it be with Cesar Romero...

TEX & BAD TEX: Hey, lemme take a good close look at you.

M C: Get away from me!—I'm dying—I am—Really—
Okay, okay, there was more but you ruined it!—
Ah—this is it—this is the end—farewell cruel world—
   nnnnnnyyyyyyyeeeeeeooooooooowwwww, boooom!
I'm dead now!
*(Actress drops M C.)*

TEX: Whattya think?

BAD TEX: Well, I'm suspicious.

TEX: Yeah I'm suspicious too.

POKE: Well, you cain't never tell about them animated creatures, boys—
Why there was a coyote round here once—

BAD TEX: Shoot—he ain't no animated creature, Poke.
He's just a stuffed animal!

*(Everyone looks at M C—no reaction.)*

BAD TEX: *(You try)*

TEX: Stuffed, heck—he's so mangy I say we just dry-clean him...

*(Everyone looks at M C—no reaction.)*

POKE: Well, whatever he is, I reckon he's gone now so I better just take him
   back to the motel and let Mister Sorehead bury him proper.

*(Exit POKE U S R, behind curtain, cowboys following)*

TEX: Whatever fer?

BAD TEX: Plot development.

TEX: Oh...

(DICK *alone in house*)

DICK: I don't know what was wrong
Maybe all the cigarette burns in the plastic
Maybe the fact that it looked like home
Maybe the fact that I was all fucked up...
I dunno.
You tell me....

(GARY *tiptoes around U S L corner of house.*)

GARY: Hey, like—what's happenin', man?

DICK: Maybe I missed the little guy...

GARY: Gary "The Nightwind" Cohen, if you're into labels
Layin down that old Mo-le-cu-lar Baseball groove...
Cause like the D N A of every hipster tripster groovy guy and groovy gal born in the lower forty-eight, Alaska, Puerto Rico and Samoa where America's day begins has encoded deep within in it all the blueprints of every stadium in the National and the American leagues...

DICK: Even the radio was beginning to sound weird....

GARY: So like kick back and shuck that chrysalis of ego dude—let's fly....

DICK: Real weird...

GARY: Flying with the Nightwind now...
*(He starts trotting around the stage.)*
Spiral-spinning down a thousand flashing neuroanatomic pathways to the cell-soul
Where the curveball hangs forever at the corner of the strikezone and there are no foreign substances,
Looking out now on the field of play...
That lovely liquid pulsing purple and magenta field
Let's just merge with it okay?
Let's all become one with the baseball inside us...
Going beyond rules, where the game becomes infinite...
I'm looking at my fingers now—
Leather webbing somehow linking them mysteriously...

GARY: The name "Ted Williams"
    written on my palm...    (DICK *crosses to window.*)
But wait—I have two hands
Wow—what's in the other
    hand?

                                      DICK: M C?

Someone sewed Humpty
    together again.

Strange need to grip                       DICK: Where are you?
Humpty Dumpty between
    my knuckles
And suddenly I'm filled with
    this amazing roaring
    sound and I'm balking,
    now,
I'm balking, but it's okay,
Because I'm floating
    upward on the roaring
    sound and as I look up
    there's a giant grey
    cigar and it's going
Goodyear...
Goodyear...                              Please come back...
Goodyear...

(GARY *exits around house;* OG *stands in far U S L corner.*)

OG: And they was three men carried up a cross
And they was three men died on Calvary that day
And they was three men carried up a cross
And they was hammered on a cross
And they was hanging on a cross
And they was dying on a cross
And they was hammered in a hand bone, hammered in a foot bone, and
    they stuck 'em in the side—great God Almighty—with an iron spike!
Three men dying up on Calvary that day and they was two men sinnermen
    and the third was Jesus Christ.
Now the one man sinner man could have been saved he could have been
    saved he could have been saved and he was *that* close to salvation till he
    mocked the Lord and went straight down to hell and he went straight to
    hell because he mocked the Lord.
And he was that close to salvation when he mocked the Lord.
But there was three men died on Calvary that day.
And the next man sinner man turn to Jesus and he call on Jesus and he call
    out help me Jesus and he cried out Lord have mercy Jesus help me in
    mine hour of death and Jesus answered Do not fear to die o do not fear
    to die this death
For I do promise you this day you shall be with me in my father's kingdom.
And the Lord cried
And the Lord cried
And the Lord cried Father help me father do not leave me father in mine

    hour of death
And the Lord died crying help me father in mine hour of death and the Lord died crying on a cross
For they were three men died on Calvary that day
And they was two men sinner men
But the third was Jesus Christ.

(POKE, *offstage, knocking at house door*)

POKE: Mister Sorehead?

DICK: Go away—whattaya want?

POKE: Wanna come in but you gotta open the door.

DICK: How come?

POKE: Got some news for you.

(POKE, *carrying shoe box, enters house, followed by cowboys.*)

DICK: You with some goddamn religious organization, too?

POKE: No, sir.
See, I'm the—call me the Lonesome—cause I been ridin' around for—goin in circles I reckon—you mind if I come in, and one other thing that I'd like to set straight before statin' my business is they call me a cowboy and not that I 'spect that they mean any harm by it mostly but still and of course I ain't one to set store on appearance but still I been hopin' or did hope I should say cause now I give it up on it mostly although I'm still hopin' in secret that someone'll notice that I am a cowgirl.
But now as to your friend he done died.

DICK: Beg your pardon?

POKE: Lookit him.

DICK: M C?

POKE: An' I'm sorry about it cause I kinda liked him despite he was full of hisself but see me and the boys we was havin' a shoot out, all friendly-like really, and then he got caught in the crossfire and died.

DICK: Can you hear me, little guy?

POKE: And I brung him so's you could bury him proper.

DICK: Please say something, M C.

POKE: You know I poked him pretty good and he warn't movin'.

DICK: Aw shoot.
I was afraid of this.
I just—I just was afraid he'd get *(Sniffles)*
Excuse me, I have this very bad sinus condition....

Poor little guy.
I'm really gonna miss him.
Now what am I gonna do.
I don't even have anything to bury him with.

POKE: You kin keep the box.

DICK: Thanks.

POKE: Tell ya—when mah horse died, course this would a been my mustang Sally cause I got a palomino now called Slow but when old Sally died it took me oh it took me days to find a big enough box cause we ain't got refrigeration in these parts and let me tell ya she got kinda stinky towards the end there!

*(By now all the other characters have crowded into the house.)*

GARY: Dearly beloved...

DICK: Uh, please, Gary.

GARY: Well, I'd like to say a few words, Dick.

DICK: Yeah, but not now, Gary.

GARY: Well, he was a friend of mine too, you know, Dick. (Asshole)
Matter of fact, he was friends with lots and lots of people, Dick
Little huddled people of every race and religion who probably never knew his name and actually never will,
And so for them, this mute and ignorant throng,
I humbly, proudly dedicate my poem....

DICK: Just keep it short, ok?

GARY: The Last At Bat—for M C Kat (by Gary Cohen)

POKE: What channel is this, anyway?

GARY: Now the stadium stands empty,
And the fans have all gone home.
The concession stands are shuttered,
And the beer has lost its foam.
And the roaring of the crowd is but a mem'ry in the ear.
For a friend of ours has left us,
Like the foam has left the beer.

Well he never had a box seat,
In the bleacher's where he'd sit.
And he never caught a pop up,
Though he always brought a mitt.
And he had so much to live for,
And you never let him drive,

And I wish to god you'd let him,
When our friend was still alive.

Well the summer days are dying,
Like a glass of beer gone flat.
In the sportsbar men are crying,
Who remember M C Kat.
But we know that he's in heaven,
And we hope he's got that glove,
And we'll join him for a cold one,
In that tap room up above....

(M C *appears as a saint in the upstage house window.*)

M C: Hey,—
Hey, what's going on?
Hey, where am I???!

GARY: Aaaarrgh!

(GARY *falls down, the rest back away from window.*)

OG: Oh, my god, it's a miracle....

M C: Am I in heaven? Oh, boy—
Hooray for MEEEE!!!!

DICK: M C?

M C: Yeah—it's me—and I'm having a religious experience—
Look at this: I can fly!

DICK: M C—what the hell do you think you're doing?

BAD TEX: Tex?

M C: Watch this—POWER DIVE!!!!

BAD TEX: Is that God, Tex?

DICK: All right, now cut it out

(DICK *exits house, followed by the rest.*)

TEX: I shore hope not.

M C: Betcha can't catch me!

DICK: Betcha you're wrong! (*Catches* M C, *takes off costume*) Come here, you...

M C: Hey, wait a minute—you can't do that—
I'm an angel!
I'm divine!
I'm the patron saint of animated creatures!

DICK: Listen, pal—you're a just a stuffed animal in a dumb looking costume so cut it out!

M C: Yeah, well everybody else thought it was pretty cool, you know....
Could probably healed the sick, raised the dead, had my own airshow...
Yeah—but you had to poop on it, didn't you?
So, okay, Mister Smarty—let's see you end the play.

DICK: Well, I don't, uh....

M C: Whatsa matter—can't come up with anything?
Where's that Wow Finish?

DICK: No, I've got ideas, I got lots of ideas, uh....

*(Enter MONICA and BOB upstage right; fade in dance music.)*

DICK: 'Course they need a little development, you know, uh...

M C: Yeah, yeah, yeah...

DICK: (Help me, damn it!)

MONICA: I alluded earlier to the benefits of trusting people....

M C: Say the magic word...

MONICA: Believe me—it's a valuable strategy.

DICK: Please...

MONICA: So begin looking for opportunities to trust people today.

DICK: Please help me...

M C: Not the magic word...

DICK: Okay...

MONICA: Let's say you don't trust the airlines to assign you a good seat

DICK: Pretty please...

M C: Nope!

MONICA: Lord knows I don't.
That's why when I get to the check-in counter I say,
"Any old seat you pick is fine with me."

M C: The magic word is: Blessed M C—hear my prayer, O Kat.
No—don't bop me!

DICK: Come back here—

M C: Wait—you're in luck—your prayers have been answered already!

*(POKE has come up to DICK, tapping him on the shoulder.)*

MONICA: And another thing—

POKE: Wanna dance, Mister Sorehead?

DICK: Uh, no, sorry, I don't...

MONICA: Be kind to yourself—

POKE: Teach ya...

MONICA: Just shut up about it!

M C: Hey—look at me, I'm dancing!

MONICA: If you have to force yourself!.

BOB: May I?

M C: Wheeeeeeeeeeee!

*(By now everyone is dancing.)*

MONICA: And so, as we reach the end, I say "Good luck"
Good luck to you
And good luck to the people who have to put up with you.
Goodnight.

END OF PLAY

*Brooklyn NY*
*29 March 1991*

www.ingramcontent.com/pod-product-compliance
Lightning Source LLC
Chambersburg PA
CBHW061254110426
42742CB00012BA/1908